Luke 10:19

"Behold, I give unto you power to tread on serpents and scorpions, and over all the power of the enemy: and nothing shall by any means hurt you."

Setting Barriers Of Fire Around Your Family Household

Strategically Formulated Tactical Combat Prayers Against Witchcraft

By: Evangelist Tony A Laurent

THE PURPOSE OF THIS BOOK

"Setting Barriers of Fire Around Your Family Household" is a powerful prayer weapon to safeguarding your family from the threats and assaults of the kingdom of darkness.

Combining practical strategies with timeless wisdom, this book emphasizes the importance of building a strong, protective foundation for your home and loved ones. Drawing from both spiritual and practical insights, it explores how to establish emotional, mental, and physical boundaries that shield your family from harm, while adopting a sense of security, unity, and resilience in spiritual warfare.

Whether you're dealing with external pressures or internal struggles, this book provides actionable prayers to ensure your household remains a sanctuary of peace and protection.

Table of Contents

Setting Barriers Of Fire Around Your Family Household
First edition. December 17, 2024.

Written by Tony A Laurent.

1. HOUSEHOLD REPENTANCE

Our Father, you who sits in the Heavens, you are creator of the heavens and the earth, You are exalted above all and in all kingdoms, spheres, realms, and dimensions of the universe.

I come before You today with a humble and contrite heart, seeking Your forgiveness for myself and on behalf of my ancestors. I acknowledge that You are a just and merciful God, full of grace and compassion, and I stand in Your presence, aware of the sins of the past that may have affected my bloodline.

Through the Blood of Y'ahushua the Lamb of God, by Your Holy Spirit and in the Name of Jesus the Christ, I now come boldly to the Throne of Grace to obtain mercy and find grace to help in this time of need.

Lord, I repent on behalf of my ancestors for any actions, decisions, or sins they committed that have brought dishonor to Your name and opened doors for curses, bondage, or separation from You. I ask for Your forgiveness for any involvement in idolatry, witchcraft, false worship, hatred, unforgiveness, injustice, or any sinful practices that have been passed down through the generations.

I renounce every generational curse, every iniquity, and every spiritual stronghold that has been inherited from my ancestors. I break every chain that has held us in spiritual bondage, and I release my family line from the consequences of these sins in the mighty name of Jesus.

Lord, I ask You to cleanse our bloodline with the precious blood of Jesus Christ. I pray that You would purify us from every defilement, every evil influence, and every wrong committed by our forefathers. I ask that you heal the wounds of the past and restore the brokenness that may have been caused by ancestral sin.

Lord, I render myself contrite and broken, and I confess and repent for the sins of my ancestral bloodline and household. I ask You to forgive us for destroying our marriage covenant. We indulged in our lust without restraint and were arrogant. We had no regard for God. We committed sinful acts and abandoned His laws. These actions caused many problems, including divorce, affairs, fornication, adultery, and unwanted pregnancies. They also led to miscommunication, quarrels, indifference, irritability, and widowed orphans. They contributed to homosexuality and bisexuality among our bloodlines.

Not only do we hurt each other, but we also hurt the children, causing great anxiety and confusion in society. Oh God! Forgive us, rescue us, and keep us away from the wicked way that is causing us to forsake, betray, and walk away from! Heal us of our deep brokenness and wounds.

Wherever my ancestors and house have participated physically or spiritually, consciously or unconsciously, directly or indirectly in any blood-drinking ceremony, blood initiation, signature agreement, ancestral worship, witchcraft meeting, occult ritual, or where we have been physically or spiritually, consciously or unconsciously, directly or indirectly initiated into conscious or subconscious witchcraft, I repent and ask for forgiveness and mercy.

Father in Heaven, forgive any member of my family bloodline who drank blood in a ritual, ingested occult foods and substances, and participated subconsciously or consciously in things associated with occultism in dreams and violated Your Word in Deuteronomy 12:23 and Leviticus 17:10.

Father, today I stand in the gap in spiritual combat to revolt against witchcraft and the diabolical forces of the 12 gates of Hell, who are seeking to keep my household from entering Heaven and fulfilling Your will and purpose.

As I engage in this tactical warfare, declaring war against the Devil's war, I request a royal pardon, forgiveness, and cleansing for my sins, iniquities, and transgressions, and for those of my family bloodline, my ancestors, and household.

Today, I repent for my sins and iniquities, both current and past, and for those of my ancestors and parents. I ask you to remove from me every stigma of sin and cleanse me from the stench of the sins of my ancestors, from my mother's house and my father's house.
Most gracious Father, I detest all personal and family transgressions and trespasses that have subjected me to become a victim of constant witchcraft afflictions and demonic harassment.

I repent for any agreement, covenant, truce, and alliance we have entered into with the kingdom of darkness, directly or indirectly, consciously or unconsciously, through my personal sins or through those of my ancestors.

By the Judicial Council of Your mercy, judgement and compassion, revive the verdict of the judicial Blood of the Lamb and the Mercy Seat, and acquit my bloodline and household of all allegations, accusations and condemnations, and of all sins, evil and wickedness embedded in me from my youth till now.

I repent for every door that my ancestors, my household, and I have opened, which allowed the demons to execute demonic spells and curses upon my household. I petition by the blood of the Lamb for Your forgiveness and cleansing through Jesus the Messiah.
Psalms 39:8, **"Deliver me from all my transgressions: make me not the reproach of the foolish"**.

By the death, burial, resurrection, and coronation of Jesus Christ as King of Kings, and through the outpouring of Your Holy Spirit, You have given me power to tread upon serpents and scorpions and over

all the powers of the enemy, and nothing shall hurt me according to Luke 10:19.
Therefore, I now put on Your power in the name of Jesus against the gates of Hell, Death, and the Grave, in the name of Jesus of Nazareth.

I declare that, by Your grace, the curse of the past is broken, and we are set free. I place our family under the covering of Your protection, and I speak blessings, healing, and restoration over our generations. Let the sins of the past no longer have authority over us, and may Your forgiveness bring freedom and renewal to my life and the lives of my descendants.

Thank you, Lord, for Your mercy and grace. Thank you for forgiving the sins of the past and making all things new. We claim the victory over every curse and every evil influence, and we choose to live in the fullness of Your blessings.

2. PRAYER AGAINST THE SPIRIT OF HOUSEHOLD DESTRUCTION

Heavenly Father, King of the ages, Omnipotent Yah who sits between the Cherubim, hallowed be Your name in all kingdoms of the heavens and the earth. Heavenly Father, indeed, You are the Most High God; Your name is holy and exalted in all kingdoms, realms, dimensions, and spheres.

By the fire of the light of God's glory, I stand in the intersection between the heavens and the earth as an intercessor for my household, and I bind, disarm, and destroy every terrestrial or psychic power using the art of metaphysical homogeneity, the channel of metaphysical intercourse, astral travel, or sound vibrations using the enigma of the four elements—water, fire, earth, and air which are used against my family household.

Therefore, in Jesus' name, I, by the verdict of the highest Order of the Council of Yah, bind, disarm, renounce, denounce, revolt against, and destroy by fire the powers and jurisdiction of the cosmological verdict of the highest council of darkness, and the power and velocity of the five Mephistophelian occult seals of demonic strongholds in my household.

O Lord my God, I request in the name of Jesus Christ, my Savior and Protector, in humility and trust, and ask for Your sovereignty and divine protection over my household against every psychic force operating in the Order of Terrestrial and Astral Hierarchies.

I also bind, disarm, destroy, and banish from over my household every power of green, blue, black, red, or white magick, harnessing the essence of creation through witchcraft formulas in order to bring destruction to my home through psychic manipulations.

I bind, disarm, and render these evil powers of destruction powerless, useless, ineffective, and defenseless against my home, in Jesus' name.

Any human or spirit agent of darkness who attempts to infiltrate the peace and safety of my household, let them be electrocuted by the lightning that emanates from Your face. Cover every door and window with the fire of the Holy Spirit, sealing them against any spiritual intrusion, demonic invasion, and nocturnal contaminations. It is written in 2 Samuel 22:15, **"And he sent out arrows, and scattered them; lightning, and discomfited them."**

Let every witch, warlock, sorcerer, wizard, grandmaster, avatar, or occult practitioner using witchcraft or esoteric arts of any kind against my household, day or night, receive fire from the coal of the altar of the God of Heaven, whose name is Yah.

Let the moon fight against them during their full moon rituals and incantations against my household.
Let the stars fight against them during their nocturnal incantation, while they use the constellations and star systems against my household in witchcraft.
Let the water fight against them as they are engaged in water witchcraft, rituals, and incantations against me and my household.
Let the fire fight against any witch who would use the fire element against me and my household in witchcraft rituals and incantations.
Let the four winds of the Earth fight against all witches who would use the air element against me in witchcraft.
Let the ground swallow any witch who would try to use the element of earth against me in witchcraft.
Let the cemetery bury any witch who would do necromancy and rituals of the dead against me in a burial ground.
Let the sun burn severely any witch who would use solar witchcraft against me and my household.

Any witch who would use thunder and lightning against me in witchcraft, let the lightning and thunder backfire upon them, as compensation with severe consequences.

Let it be as I have spoken, for it is written in Isaiah 44:26, **"That confirms the word of his servant, and performs the counsel of his messengers;"**

I strike all powers of darkness with extreme and severe friction burns, cold burns, thermal burns, radiation burns, chemical burns, and electrical burns by the fiery presence of the Lord Jesus and His Angels. All evil powers within the darkness who are fighting my household with sustained diffusion of destructive psychic attacks, let them be roasted to dry ash, in Jesus name.

I declare by the jurisdiction of the blood of Jesus, no member of my household will be a sacrifice of any kind to the deities and demigods of the occult world of the land, sea, air, or underworld.

None of my offspring or members of my household will be a sacrifice to Moloch, or to the god of thunder, the god of death, the god of the forests, the god of the serpents, or the gods of the shrines, or the god of witchcraft.

Defend my household from the Avatars and Living Grand Masters, who operate by the Inner Esoteric framework and the Hierarchy of the powers of darkness, within the Astral and Terrestrial dimension.

Bring judgement upon the 400,000 categories of psychic strongholds and entities, set in astral motion against my household. Judge the entities of the 'Inner Esoteric' framework and the Hierarchy of the powers of the Astral and Terrestrial dimension.

You have given me authority to fight against the powers of darkness and prevail, and have anointed me with the fire to disarm the powers of darkness.

Today, in Your holy name, I declare war against household destruction in the name of the Lord.
I call upon the Pillar of Fire by night and the Pillar of Cloud by day, to divide between the satanic operations of the nighttime and the satanic operations of the daytime. Let my household be covered by the rays of Your lightning and fire, O Adonai Tzevaot, the Lord God of hosts.

Every midnight terror, or arrows of the midday gate of the sun, pestilence that walks in darkness and destruction at noon that is set for my household, I call destruction upon these evil forces.

Let the forces of the Twilight Zone and the Gates of the Dawn who falsify my household blessings and success and increase be banished by the fire of God's holy altar.

Let my household be protected by lightning and fire, by the verdict of the council of the Almighty God, against every mighty vicious spirit being from the third psychic realm of the air.

Let the terror and the dregs of the cup of the fury of Almighty God terrorize all evil guardians of the flame, who would try to launch satanic assaults against my household using various schemes and strategies from the Book of Technique, tactic, Grimoire, and any other Satanic script containing deadly formulas for destruction.

In the name of Jesus of Nazareth, I call destructive terror and degradation upon all evil forces of combined elements of astral spirits, sustaining a one thousand and ninety-five-day cycle attack against my household.

In the mighty name of the Messiah Jesus, Son of God, I place every witchcraft operation in my life under the fiery judgement of God written in Deut 18:10-12.

It is written in Psalms 60:12, **"Through God I shall do valiantly; for He it is that shall tread down our enemies."**

Every satanic assault that is launched against my household from any coven, occult zone, region, or center, let these be neutralized, as I apply the force of prayer against them.

In the name of Jesus, I call forth an angelic encampment around my household with flames of lightning, and let every evil structure, demonic fortress, witchcraft monument, and cage explode to pieces.

Let there be light in my home, and let darkness and its associates be dispelled now, in Jesus' name. For it is written in Psalms 144:6, **"Cast forth lightning, and scatter them: shoot out thine arrows, and destroy them."**
Surround my household, O Lord, with Your mighty warring angels, Your protecting angels, Your mounting angels, Your linking angels, Your ministering angels, and Your angels of wind and fire, and set Your chariots of divine flames round about every member of my household.
Your Word says that no weapon formed against me shall prosper, and I claim that promise over my household.

Therefore, I rebuke any spirits of destruction, chaos, calamity, or harm and disaster that seek to enter my household. By the authority given to me through Jesus Christ, I command every evil force to leave this place immediately and never return.

It is written in Psalms 71:13, **"Let them be confounded and consumed that are adversaries to my soul; let them be covered with reproach and dishonour that seek my hurt."**

By the authority of my salvation in Jesus Christ, I pray that all evil powers seeking to swallow up my house in chaos let themselves swallow themselves instead.

Gates of good opportunities that were shut to my household swing open now, in Jesus' name.

Every turbulence in the air that is programmed to fight against the blessings of my household for a cycle of 364 days be neutralized now in Jesus' name.

By fire, lightning, and thunder, in the name of Y'ahushua, I pull out the life, the destiny, the health, the mind, the career, the glory, the anointings, the ministry, the souls, the star, the success, business, future, and wealth of my household from the Bermuda Triangle, from the Mediterranean Sea, the Adriatic Sea, the Black Sea, the Red Sea, the Sargasso Sea, the Arabian Sea, the Caspian Sea, the Baltic Sea, the Persian Gulf, and from the North Atlantic Ocean, the South Atlantic Ocean, the North Pacific Ocean, the South Pacific Ocean, the Arctic Ocean, the Southern Ocean, the Indian Ocean, and from the Congo River, the River Nile, the Mississippi River, the Amazon River, the Orinoco River, the St. Lawrence River, the Niger River, and all lesser rivers, where the life of the members of my household was thrown through witchcrafts.

Traps and snares set for my household by ambushment, using tactical procedures by the serpents and scorpions, are smashed to powder and nothingness, in Jesus' name. It is written in Psalms 27:2, **"When the wicked, even mine enemies and my foes, came upon me to eat up my flesh, they stumbled and fell."**

I decree by the decree of the Blood of Jesus and the Council of the Most High, and I say, my household will not be food or meat for water nymphs, mermaids, necro-demons, zombie spirits, or sirens; neither will the blood of my household be drink for witchcraft festivals, feasts, or rituals. .

Let every witch, warlock, sorcerer, wizard, or occult practitioner working witchcraft of any form against me, during this daylight, receive fire, and sustain extreme and severe friction burns, cold burns, thermal burns, radiation burns, chemical burns, and electrical burns from the fiery presence of the Lord Jesus and His Angels, as I have spoken it, for it is written in Isaiah 44:26, **"That confirms the word of His servant, and performs the counsel of His messengers;"**

kingdom of darkness using the sunlight against me, I pray against it through the power of Yahusha of Nazareth.

I now invoke a Divine Judicial Order from the Courts of the Almighty God, who is the Grand Judge of the Heavens and the Earth, and I command by this Divine Judicial Order that there be rest and peace in my family household, with an immediate release of joy unspeakable and full of glory.

I pray for wisdom to make wise decisions in maintaining and securing my household, and I pray, Lord Jesus, that you strengthen its foundations, both physical and spiritual.

I pray for discernment to recognize any subtle attacks and wisdom to take preventive measures. Fill our hearts with Your love and peace, that we may dwell securely in Your presence.

Father, thank you for listening to me and delivering my household from evil and setting us free, so that we can glorify You in all wisdom.

Thank you, Father, for your protection and faithfulness.

I pray these prayers in no other name but the name of Y'ahushua HaMashiach, for thine is the kingdom, the power, and the glory forever. Amen and Amen.

3. BRINGING THE CHILDREN TO THE ALTAR OF GOD

Heavenly Father, King of the universe, Omnipotent God who is, who was, and who is to come. Hallowed be Your name in all kingdoms of the heavens and the earth, for You are the Most High God; Your name is holy and exalted in all kingdoms, realms, dimensions, and spheres.

Lord of hosts, you said in Mark 10:14, **"But when Jesus saw it, he was much displeased, and said unto them, Suffer the little children to come unto me, and forbid them not: for of such is the kingdom of God."**
Through the sanctification of my children through the believing parents, I bring my children before Your sapphire Throne in prayer, requesting that you bless my children and deliver them from the holds of the kingdom of darkness. My children/child [CALL THEIR NAMES] belong to the kingdom of God.

I petition you, Lord Jesus, by Your Holy Spirit, that you protect my child/children [CALL THEIR/HIS/HER NAME] and lay Your holy hands upon them, for it is written in Matthew 19:13-15, **"Then were there brought unto him little children, that he should put his hands on them and pray."**

Destroy all diabolical strategies and satanic traps from the book "Technique Tactics", Grimoire, or the Book of the Dead that are being used against them/him/her. Protect them/him/her from the lowest to the highest level of diabolical assaults projecting from the Book of Grimoire and the Book of the Dead and destroy every Satanic formula for death and destruction that is sent against them/him/her.

Every evil power within any of the seven main kingdoms of darkness working through vicious arts of sorcery to subject any of my children or household family members to become a compensation sacrifice, a collateral sacrifice, a replacement sacrifice, or freewill sacrifice to a deity or demon, I cancel and destroy the evil plans, power, force, and velocity of these evil powers in the name of Jesus the Christ.

I loose my household from every chain of witchcraft, affliction, shackle, chain, torment, and padlock of death, by accident, death in sleep, sudden death, or death by bullets, knife, cutlass, vehicle, drowning, or sickness.
I declare by the blood of Jesus, no member of my household, nor any of my children, will be sacrificed to devils or demons.

Lord, you have given me authority to fight against the powers of darkness and prevail; and have anointed me with the fire to disarm the powers of darkness on behalf of my child/children.
Right now, by Your Holy Spirit, I stand in the capacity of my parental authority and petition that You clothe me with Your light and fire, so that I can stand in prayer and warfare for my children this day against the diabolical system of the gates of Hell.

Today, by the jurisdiction of the Blood of the Lamb of God, in the holy name of Elohei Tzeva'ot and El-Gibbor, I declare war against all the hosts of darkness who have been programmed to fight against my children.
I pray against every working of Satan, and the operation of the prince of darkness and their subordinate spirits, working within the Mephistophelian seals, and the degree of psychic strongholds in order to lay chains of demonic afflictions upon my children and their children and children's children.

By my authority in Christ, by chains of vehement flames of the holiness of Jesus Christ of Nazareth, I bind, disarm, and neutralize every demon of death, demon head-hunter, demon reaper, and all destroyer demons, etc., who are sent to annihilate and kill my child/children physically in any way.

I strike every sniffing and scent-chasing demon with parosmia and render them incapable of detecting the body odours of my children and household, in Jesus' mighty name.

Any of my children who are placed on death row by the kingdom of the Occult and Demons, I deliver this child from death row this minute, by the power of Jesus of Nazareth, and I destroy the band and hold of Hades from over my child/children now, effective immediately, in the exalted name of Jesus of Nazareth.

I also remove my children's names from the death register of the Underworld, and I scatter and liquidate by fire all combined elements of astral poisons working together to bring about the specific task and mission of implementing premature death, sudden death, slow death, and death by accident upon my child/children.

I now call upon the fiery lightning of the holy presence of the Lord Jesus to burn out all evil marks, identifications, occult names, sigils, and the date of my children's death that have been placed upon their foreheads, in Jesus' Name.

I withdraw my children's names from every tombstone, gravestone, grave, cemetery, and I pray that any tombstone or headstone in the spirit realm, upon which the name, the date of birth, and the date of death of my child/children are inscribed, by the power of the name of

Jesus, I demolish and shatter this gravestone to powder; let it be blown to pieces now!

I invoke the lightning of the invisible destructive fire from Almighty God in Heaven to shatter any coffin into debris that was constructed for any of my children in the astral realm through witchcraft.
I tear to threads any grave clothes tailored specifically for my child/children in the occult realm. I say you are a liar; catch fire and be consumed to ashes now in Jesus' mighty name.

I neutralize every astral poison, astral motion, astral venom, and psychic vibration and sound frequency, and destroy the powers of the elemental spirits. In the name of Jesus, the Christ of Nazareth, may these evil forces backfire in the face of the grand demon in charge of these attacks. Amen!

All astral poison and venom of tranquilization and neutralization that have neutralized my children, so that they cannot function with precise intellectual capacities, pristine intelligence, and pristine articulation of their expression of morals, self-worth, integrity, knowledge, and love for Jesus, release my children's lives and potential now.

Every subtle psychic manipulation by witchcraft, necromancy, injuring, conjuring, projecting, voodoo herb mixture, incantation, ritual, altar, and every plot, plan, weapon, curse, snare, lair, or any other esoteric craft deployed to destroy any of my children shall be met with incomprehensible destruction by fire and shall be roasted to dry ash, vaporized by fire, and vanished into thin air without a trace. In the mighty name of Jesus.

I neutralize you, Demon of venom, and reclaim the full functionality of my children's faculties—intellectually, spiritually, emotionally, psychologically, mentally, by fire and by the authority of the Blood of Jesus and the power of the seven horns of the Lamb of God in Revelation 5:6.

By lightnings and thunders of fire wrapped in the glory of the eternal light of Christ, I gather the fragments of my children's souls from every realm, sphere, occult zone, region, center, and dimension of the upper darkness and lower darkness, in Jesus' name.

Every crocodilian, reptilian, and serpentine spirit that has swallowed my children in realms and spheres of darkness, despair, and gloom, I release a detonation inside your bowels now, and shatter to bits and pieces the prison holds that are holding my children in realms and spheres of darkness, despair, and gloom.

By the power of the Holy Spirit of Jesus Christ, I take up as my companion the light, lightning, and thunder of the presence of Jesus, the King of Kings, and I now enter into all realms where the spirits of my children are trapped, and I declare a divine rescue.

In the name of Jesus of Nazareth, by the God of Noah, Abraham, Moses, Daniel, Job, and Elijah, with fire and force, I burst every iron bar asunder and destroy every bronze gate, and all energy forces that are trapping the spirits of my children within the realm of witchcraft.

I declare wars of fire against all demons and Fallen angels. By the power of Jesus Christ, and in the name of the Lord God of Host, I pull out my Children's spirits from any land of darkness, the valley of death's shadows, any underground cave, astral labyrinth, cemetery, spiritual maze, catacomb, demonic pit, trench, slum, and any spiritual jail cell, desert, water, and air. I also pull them from any underground astral chamber, wastelands, barren lands, desolate places, woodlands, wetlands, enchanted forest, monsoon forest, tropical forest, swamp, sacred grove, mangrove, everglades, and from any catacomb, grave, crossroad, fork road, roundabout, metropolitan, megapolitan, town, urban area, state, and nation.

I speak with fire to every realm, category, and rank of witchcraft, and I say powers of witchcraft be broken, destroyed, nullified, and banished, and release the spirits of my children now, effective immediately, in Jesus name.
I barricade my children with barriers of electric fire, and permanent walls of reinforced resistance and defenses of lightning and light.

It is written in Psalm 27:2, **"When the wicked, even mine enemies and my foes, came upon me to eat up my flesh, they stumbled and fell."**
It is written in Psalms 71:13, **"Let them be confounded and consumed that are adversaries to my soul; let them be covered with reproach and dishonour that seek my hurt."**
By the invisible fire of the Almighty God in Heaven, which is mixed with brimstone, tempest, lightning, thunders and hail, I destroy any coffin that was constructed for any of my children in the astral realm through witchcraft, in the name of Jesus. Arrows of slow death, fired into the body of my children, be removed by the power of Jesus.

Demon of failure, setback, and stagnation retarding the spiritual growth of my children, [call your children's name], be shattered to pieces by holy lightning according to Psalm 18:14.
Arrows of the Almighty God in Psalms 18:14, locate my children's enemies who are working evil against them. Let my children's enemies be scattered and be rendered in grievous shame and disgrace now, in Jesus' name.

Powers of the air feeding on my children's destiny, by the invisible fire of the Almighty God in Heaven, and with brimstone, tempest, lightning, thunders, and hail, I destroy and banish you evil spirits from my children's lives, effective immediately, in Jesus name.

Power of the grave, the graveyard, tombstones, and catacombs, created and marked for any of my children, I render your power impotent, frustrated, nullified, barren, ineligible, and useless in the lives of my children, in the name of Jesus.

Any evil poison, potion, or enchanted substance from the dead, the dark aquatic kingdom, or any other dark realm, given to any of my children to eat or drink by psychic travel, through a magic mirror portal, or in a dream; and every demon implanted in my children by these substances. I command these astral poisons to be neutralized and flushed from my children's bodies and souls, effective immediately.
Let these creatures in the belly, spine, sacral region, or any other part of my children's bodies become powerless, impotent, frustrated, barren, illegal, and useless, and be banished by the power of the blood of Jesus and the throne of Jesus Christ.

Any sickness planted in the bodies of my children while sleeping, or through any spiritual food or water, or any point of contact, be flushed out by the blood of Jesus, the power, and the name of Jesus of Nazareth.

I liquidate, dissolve, nullify, and dispel every demonic or satanic alliance, relationship, covenant, connection, and partnership that was made with my children or any of my children through contact, association, or dream, astral soul travel, or through magic mirrors, now in the name of Jesus of Nazareth.
Every witchcraft power that has placed and imprisoned the spirit of my child/children inside a burial tomb, underground chamber, bottle, vase, witch bag, black box, tree, rock, maze, or any other item or

realm, I destroy these evil holds and prisons, and by the power of Jesus Christ, I set the spirits of my children free from all demonic captivities.

I address you demons of captivity, and I now place you into captivity by the blood of Jesus and fire, for it is written, captivity shall go into captivity. You have no power to hold my child or children any longer. Therefore, all you evil forces of captivity by witchcraft, be shattered by lightning and power of Jesus Christ now, in Jesus' name.

No witchcraft curse by the hands of the Secret Cult or Satanic Coven will terminate the lives of my children in the name of Jesus.
Every agent of darkness seeking to drink the blood of my children, I say these evil agents of darkness will drink their own blood by force and stifle in the process, in the name of Jesus.
Death, I rebuke your hands from over my children by the power of the death, burial, and resurrection of Jesus Christ of Nazareth. My children are not your victims, nor are they your candidates; therefore, hand of death, be removed from over my children now, in the name of Jesus of Nazareth.

I retrieve my children's memory, ability, and potential from the chambers of the Marine kingdom and every place where their memory is being held incarcerated. By fire, I also retrieve my children's memory, ability, and potential from the den of thieves and every marketplace of Hell.

I command the Fire of the Holy Spirit in the secret places of the mysterious kingdom of darkness, and all storerooms, vessels, chambers, or anything that is holding my children's memory, name, and destiny trapped.
I command these evil forces to melt by the Fire of El-Eliyahu, in Jesus' Name. Let every creature who has stolen or is stealing from my children be roasted by the fire of amber proceeding from the throne

of Jesus Christ. Let terror, fire, and brimstone come upon all evil for my children's sake now, in the name of Jesus of Nazareth.

Any of my children who may have been initiated from the mother's womb or shortly after birth, or growing up, I nullify and denounce this initiation as void, redundant, and useless. I destroy this initiation and the agents of darkness who are responsible for this initiation; let them be burned by the unquenchable holy Fire of Yahuah, El-Shaddai. In Jesus Name.

Blood that was taken from my children for testing, which was used by occultists, witches, grand masters, satanic midwives, and nurses, occult doctors, and laboratory personnel, I plead the verdict of the blood of Jesus into this past reality and destroy every witchcraft placed on my children.

Wherever my children's blood is being held in darkness, let it vanish now in Jesus' name, and the chamber where the blood is held be destroyed by fire beyond recognition, now in Jesus' name.

I also pray that every demon of land, sea, and air; every water, land, and cemetery dragon, every serpent of the waters and dry places, every demonic wild beast and creature who has drunk the blood of our children or child in the hospital, in dream. Or astral projection, or sexual violation in sleep, I command, in the Name of Jesus of Nazareth that these children's haemoglobin, lifeforce, and destiny be vomited up now, and all you evil creatures catch fire and roast to powder now, by the fire of El- Eliyahu, in Y'ahushua's Name.

My **daughters** *will be* **as cornerstones, polished** *after* **the similitude of a palace: according to"** **Psalms** 144:12, for it is written, "That **our sons** *may be* **as plants grown up in their youth;** *that* our **daughters** *may be* **as cornerstones, polished** *after* **the similitude of a palace:"**

Wherever I have built a godly and holy altar, cause my children to have an encounter there like Jacob, who had an encounter where Abraham built an altar in Luz.

Let my children be taught the mechanics of things that will build them for future events through the power of Jesus Christ of Nazareth and give my children divine intelligence.
Lord God, teach my children the dynamics of time and seasons.
Teach my children the dynamics of the Word of God,
Teach my children the dynamics of fervent prayer.
Teach my children the dynamics of economizing.
Teach my children the dynamics of fervency.
Teach my children the dynamics of strong faith.
Teach my children the dynamics of fasting.
Teach my children the dynamics of cultivation.
Teach my children the dynamics of skills.

Lord, I pray that You make all things are possible.

Thank You, Father, for Your constant presence and guidance. I trust in Your perfect plan for my life and education. In all things, may I honour You and seek Your glory, in Jesus' name Amen and Amen.

4. PRAYER FOR THE SPIRIT OF EXCELLENCE IN YOUR HOUSEHOLD EDUCATION

Heavenly Father, my heart is filled with gratitude for the opportunity to learn and grow. Thank You for the gift of education and the ability to acquire knowledge and wisdom in this world, as we occupy till You come.
I know that You are the source of all wisdom, and I seek Your guidance, educational favour, and blessings in the educational journey of my household.

In the name of Jesus of Nazareth, I pray that the gift of education and the grace to attain great education in all fields will come upon, rest, and abide in my household.

I invoke the spirit of excellence upon all members of my household, that they will possess an excellent spirit and wisdom beyond their years.
I speak into the atmosphere of my household, and I say by the jurisdiction of the holy altar, education shall not fail in my household.

Heavenly Father, I am asking for your guidance and blessing on my children's minds. Grant them a sharp memory, the ability to retain information clearly, and the focus to recall important details when needed. Help them to store knowledge in their hearts and minds, and to access it readily when necessary. Guide them to use their memory wisely and to always honor You in their thoughts and actions.

Lord, I ask for Your divine assistance in all their studies. Please grant my household impeccable understanding, clarity, and focus as we seek to learn. Remove any distractions that would hinder my progress and fill my mind with the ability to absorb and retain what we have been taught. The memory of my children is blessed.

I speak and decree by the Holy Spirit of Fire, all members of my household are bred for signs and wonders and are fashioned as vessels of honour, of high esteem, pillars of knowledge, and holders of honorary certificates and graduates of high degrees.

O God Almighty, plant in the life of my household the power to gain knowledge, the wisdom to structure the components of success, the understanding to harness the substance of instruction and intelligence. May the oil of the seven pillars of wisdom be poured upon the members of my household so that they can represent You on the earth.

I pray against destiny hunters, destiny eaters, and destiny destroyers, who have also created crooked things and crooked paths in the life of my household in order to destroy their educational success and opportunities.

I throw into oblivion the spirit of educational failures, educational mishaps, educational disgrace, educational frustrations, lags, glitches, misunderstandings, and distastefulness that have rested or are seeking to rest upon my household.

Let these cycles of educational failure that plagued my ancestors not repeat themselves in my household, in Jesus' name.

I retrieve the education of my household from all terrestrial realms, sub-aquatic regions, astral layers, occult plains, zones, regions, and kingdoms, or from any glass jar, iron or bronze vessel, black box, wooden box, iron box, or from any tree root, calabash, vase, altar, shrine, river, sea, pond, pool, or lake, and from any of the five occult zones of the marine kingdom: the zones Lumani, Banni, Lemuria, Gamma, and the occult zone of Atlantis, or any other place where my household's education is held captive.

I call forth the fire of El Eliyahu to descend and dry up all evil waters of educational barrenness and unfruitfulness flowing into my household from the evil fountains of my ancestral foundations.

I declare war on any spirits of the python, crocodilian, anaconda, reptilian, or serpentine kind that are fighting against my household's success in education.

I also declare war against any python, crocodilian, dragon, anaconda, reptilian, or serpentine spirits that have swallowed the educational success and accomplishments of the members of my household.

By a divine judicial court order, I invoke the verdict of the Almighty God in Joel 2, and I command all spirits who have swallowed the education of my household to restore it sevenfold, now in Jesus' name.

By power, I pry the jaws of these evil beasts open and retrieve my household education in Jesus' name.

By the authority of Jesus Christ and the power of the Holy Spirit of Jesus, we condemn every condemnation laid over my household by the grand juror of the Judicial Court of the kingdom of darkness, by the attorney general of Hell, the jurors of the high council of darkness, by the magistrate of esoteric forces, and by the high Judge of the Devil's kingdom.

Your word says, O Lord, in Psalms 94:21, **"They gather themselves together against the soul of the righteous and condemn innocent blood."**

Those who are gifted to be doctors in my household, I call into fruition and purpose, in Jesus' name.

I call into fruition and purpose anyone in my household who is gifted to be an Apostle, Prophet, Evangelist, Pastor, or Teacher. They are a steward, oracle, and pillar in the five-fold ministry of the Apostolic, in Jesus' name.

I call into fruition anyone in my household who is gifted to be a doctor, engineer, nurse, biologist, chemist, social scientist, pilot, or skilled worker, etc. I do this for the purpose of fulfilling their gifts, in Jesus' name.

I pray against the displacement and replacement of the education of the members of my household. Wherever their education has been captured and locked up within.

I pray and command the educational destiny, prosperity, and wealth to surface from where they are held captive and be restored to my life sevenfold.

Let every watery environment and chaos surrounding my prosperity and financial wealth dry up now, by the power of Jesus Christ.

Lord Jesus, help my family and household to work diligently and wisely, to manage our time effectively, and to approach our studies with a spirit of excellence.

Lord, I pray that You would bless my efforts and lead me to success. May my education not only be for personal achievement but also for the purpose of serving You and others. I commit all my goals, dreams, and studies to You, knowing that with Your help, all things are possible.

Thank You, Father, for Your constant presence and guidance. I trust in Your perfect plan for my life and education. In all things, may I honour You and seek Your glory, in Jesus' name Amen and Amen

5. INVOKINIG SERAPHIC MINISTRY IN THE FINANCES OF YOUR HOUSEHOLD

Lord our God, King of the ages, All-powerful and All-mighty, who sits between the Cherubim of burning coals, hallowed be Your name in all the kingdoms of the heavens and the earth.

1 Chronicles 29:10, "**Blessed** *are* **You, LORD God of Israel our Father, forever and ever.**
Vs.11, "**O LORD, Yours** *is* **the greatness, and the power, and the glory, and the victory, and, the majesty, for all in the heavens and in the earth** *is Yours.* **Yours** *is* **the kingdom, O LORD, and You are exalted as head over all.**"
Vs.12, "**And the riches and the honour** *are* **from You, and You reign over all. And in Your hand** *is* **power and might. And** *it is* **in Your hand to make great and to give strength to all.**"

Today I give You praise, honour, and glory, as I now come with boldness to Your fiery throne of grace, made of sapphire, seeking Your holy intervention in the matter of the finances of my family household, according to Hebrews 4:16 and Philippians 4:6. Lord, the wealth, prosperity, and finances of my household have been ambushed by astral spirits of hell, who have purposed to steal, kill, and destroy. But heavenly Father, You are the Most High God. Your name is holy, and You are exalted in all kingdoms, realms, dimensions, and spheres.

· **Repentance For Ancestral Financial Wickedness**
I repent for every sin, abomination, and evil that is in my family's financial foundation. Every sin of theft, robbery, unjust merchandising (Pro 20:10, Hosea 12:7-8) that is embedded in my life and family, O Lord, acquit my life and household from these allegations, accusations, and condemnations through the blood of Jesus.

Lord, your word says in Ezekiel 22:27, **"Her princes in the midst thereof *are* like wolves ravening the prey, to shed blood, to destroy souls, and to get dishonest gain."**
At any point in time in history where my ancestors or current family household have gained ungodly riches, wealth, and financial fame at the expense of another person's life, health, or livelihood (Pro 1:19), I repent for these evils and wickedness, and I ask for pardon, redemption, and deliverance for my bloodline, of both my mother's house and my father's house.

Wherever the curses of finances are sitting upon my life and my family household because of wealth gained by wickedness, and an alliance made with the personification of covetousness, murder, ambush, human trafficking, human sacrifice, etc., may the light of fire break every satanic power of financial curse from over us now, in Jesus' name.

I plead with your divine council, O Lord of Heaven, and request through the Blood of the new covenant of Christ that my household be set free from this hold of evil, financial condemnation, lack, and poverty.

Your word says in Proverbs 15:27, **"He that is greedy of gain troubleth his own house; but he that hateth gifts shall live."**
I confess, renounce, reject, and denounce every curse, iniquity, and sin of greed that is troubling my household and stemming from the ungodly financial pillars of my ancestral foundation.

• Petitioning The Courts of God

Heavenly Father, your face is made of light, fire, and lightning, from which light is emitted and enlightens the entire sphere of the heavens and the earth. You sit upon the throne of electric fire of amber, and dwell between two Cherubim of burning coals, where there are flowing rivers of living fire moving between and among the Seraphim and Ophannim in the tenth heaven.

Master, all dimensions, realms, spheres, and kingdoms bow before Your Majesty and Sovereignty.
I come to your holy courts, where the fire of your love, mercy, and compassion is the platform upon which your justice is rendered and served in favour of the saints, through the blood of Jesus.

Oh Lord, Your secret place is a place by You [Exo 33:21]. Let Your inner sanctum, holiness, and fire answer my petition by fire, and bring my prayers into Your Inner Chamber of light and glory.
Sanctify my prayer request to approach Your throne of grace in the courts of Heaven and find help from Your divine council in the Inner Chambers of Your sanctuary.

Heavenly Saviour and God, I request today that the Divine Council of the Almighty God, who is the Grand Judge of the Heavens and the Earth, be seated for my sake and that of my household, and let my cause now be brought before the Lord of all the Earth.

Your Majesty, I am requesting a divine judicial order that everything the kingdom of darkness has stolen and taken from my life and that of my household in the areas of wealth, success, prosperity, and finances be restored to me sevenfold, effective immediately.

I request today that the Divine Council of the Almighty God, who is the Grand Judge of the Heavens and the Earth, be seated for my sake and that of my household, and let my supplication be brought to Your holy court of petition.

Lord God, I request of your holy Council the intervention of your Seraphim (or burning ones) to specifically burn to ashes every tribal and ancestral tie and knot that is constraining, restricting, and retarding my finances and those of my household.

Let the Seraphim purge and destroy from my family bloodline all ancient corruptions, evil ties, tribal spiritual alliances, and iniquities of financial wickedness.

I am requesting that the fire of the eternal flame of love, mercy, compassion, power, and the Word of God descend upon my household to purify and sanctify the finances of my household from all evil, impurities, desecration, and ancient and modern abominations.

Send fire from heaven to retrieve my finances and those of my household from the house of the gods, the shrines of idols, the temple of ancient deities, renowned gods and goddesses, from the altar of ancient evil personifications, and from the hand of the entities of the scum of darkness.

Intervene, O God of Hosts, by lightning and thunder, for it is written in Psalms 81:7, **"You called in trouble, and I delivered you; I answered you in the secret place of thunder."**
It is written in 2 Samuel 22:17-18, **"He sent from above, he took me; he drew me out of many waters; He delivered me from my strong enemy, *and* from them that hated me: for they were too strong for me."**

• Waging War For Your Finances

I declare warfare of destruction upon all the esoteric forces, and the psychic forces within the cosmic sea, the astral layers, and the underground occult regions that have caused demons to carry out financial curses upon me and my household, directly or through witchcraft vibrations.

In the name of Jesus of Nazareth, I pray against and destroy by the power of the name and verdict of the fire of the blood of Christ, the effectiveness, astral rights, and operations of the Mephistophelian land occult Seal 333, and all operations of the cosmological verdict of the Inner Esoteric framework within the Celestial Sanctum, which have captured or are fighting against the finances of my household.

Today, Lord Jesus, I place my finances before Your altar.
Destroy now, O God of hosts, Elohei Tzeva'ot, the archspirits and lesser forces of the etheric sphere within the occult grand divisions in the mystical world of darkness, who have armed, sworn oaths, and purposed themselves to destroy my finances at all costs.

Lord Jesus of Nazareth, may the God of the Heavens and the Earth arise as He arose upon Mount Perazim, and scatter the enemies of my household right now, in Your holy name, Yahusha HaMashiach.
For it is written in Isaiah 28:21, **"For the LORD shall rise up as *in* mount Perazim, he shall be wroth as *in* the valley of Gibeon, that he may do his work, his strange work; and bring to pass his act, his strange act."**

With lightnings and the seven voices of the secrets of thunders, pour out the fiery coals of amber from beneath the secret places of your altar, and cleanse my finances from any demonic symbiotic substance or blood of the innocent that has been placed on my finances as a stigma of financial degradation and destruction.

I call down thunderstorms of fire and lightning upon every witch, warlock, Satanist, ritualist, witch doctor, native doctor, and voodoo priest who has been or is currently destroying my financial life and that of my household. I command the trenches of the earth to swallow these occult practitioners and cast them into oblivion and obscure darkness for a season, in Jesus' name.

I declare wars of fire, lightning, and thunder in the heavens above, and in the earth beneath against all high demons of the underworld associated with wealth and money, who are influencing, eating, sitting, and destroying my finances.

I destroy and banish from my finances and the finances of my household the influence, power, essence, aura, and curse of the spirits of the goddess Juno or *Moneta and the* gods Mammonae, Plutus, Pluto, Hades, Orcus, and Dis Pater, and the forces of the genies.

In the name of Jesus and by the power of the God who rides upon the heavens by His name Yah, I loose and unlock my finances and those of my household from wherever they are bound by darkness.

By the power of Jesus Christ given to me in Luke 10:19, and by the power of 1Samuel 30:8, **"Pursue: for thou shalt surely overtake them, and without fail recover all,"** I retrieve by the fire of amber my finances and wealth from the waste places, from the gutter, the drains, sewer, lake, swamp, pond, toilet, from the trenches, the scum, from any river, "tributary," "estuary," "strait," "channel," "canal," "fjard," "bay," "gulf," "fjord," "bight," "sound," "cove," "inlet," "polynya," or from the forest, desert, cemetery, black box, enchanted jar.

By the power of Jesus Christ given to me in Luke 10:19 and 1Samuel 30:8, I recover and retrieve by the fire my finances and wealth from any iron or bronze vessel, wooden box, iron box, or from any tree root, calabash, vase, altar, shrine, sea, pond, pool, or lake, and from any of the five occult zones of the marine kingdom: the zones Lumani, Banni, Lemuria, Gamma, and the occult zone of Atlantis, or from the Sargasso Sea, the Bermuda Triangle, or any other place where my household finances are held captive, effective immediately.

I remove my finances and those of my household from the evil hands of the demon of perpetual destruction and the genies, water sirens, from the male and female supreme mermaids (the Huna and the Huni), and the elemental spirits of the land, forest, water, fire, and air.

I destroy their powers over my household's finances, with immediate effect, all their jurisdiction over our lives, in the name of Jesus of Nazareth.

I disassemble, scatter, and liquidate the forces of the combined elements of astral entities that are destroying my finances and those of my household.

I command that all that was stolen from me and my household be set free, rise to the surface, and be recovered from the hands of the seven kingdoms of darkness.

Let fire now descend from the seven altars of Jesus in heaven, and destroy every dragon, serpent, python, beast, anaconda, giant, or creature of hell that is holding my finances in its belly.

I call upon the God of Jeshurun, who rides upon the heaven in my help, in his excellency on the sky [Deut 33:26], and by faith I say let the Angel Micha'el, Gabri'el, Rapha'el, and Uri'el place a hook of brass and iron in the jaw and nostril of every Dragon, Serpent, Python, Beast, and Anaconda from the fresh and salty waters, land, and air that have swallowed the wealth and finances of my household, and let my finances be retrieved from their bellies.

I invoke the lightning of fire and dangerous thunders and fiery brimstones of terror upon all demons, sirens, and angels who are carrying the wealth, finances, and prosperity of my household in their hands or within their bodies.

All evil creatures of the occult world who are programmed, mandated, and scheduled to fight against my household finances' prosperity, let the Angels of the Lord of hosts drag out these Dragons, Serpents, Pythons, beasts, creatures, and Anacondas from their hiding places, binding them in chains of fire to the dry, hot sand of the desert.

Let these evil creatures destroying my finances be persecuted by the flames of the sun seven times, and let the creatures of the desert devour them in the mighty name of Jesus.

Holy Father, I pray in the presence of Your Holy Spirit that I will shout for joy and be glad that You will favour my righteous cause: yea, and let me say continually, let the LORD be magnified, which hath pleasure in the prosperity of His servant. [Psalms 35:27].

Therefore, through the authority of the altar of divine Flames and the holy Blood of Jesus the Lamb, I loose the financial bands and I open the gates of treasures, in the heavens and the earth, and I command the gates of wealth and financial favours to be unlocked unto my household, from the North, South, East, and West. I now invoke rains of blessings upon my household, in Jesus name.

By the grand order of the verdict of the Blood of the New Covenant of Christ, I charge every treasury of finances and wealth in all four corners of the heavens and the earth to channel into my life a great flow of accumulated finances and wealth, without interruption and delay, effective immediately.

Lord, You know the desires of my heart, and You know my every need before I pray [Mat 6:32]. Not one sparrow falls to the ground without Your knowledge [Mat 10:29]. You clothed the lilies of the field [Mat 6:28-29] and planted the fir trees in which all the birds of the air lodge therein.

I say today according to Psalms 104:17, "The trees of the LORD are full of sap; the cedars of Lebanon, which he hath planted; where the birds make their nests: as for the stork, the fir trees are her house. The high hills are a refuge for the wild goats; and the rocks for the conies." [Psalms 104:16-18].

Your word says in Matthew 6:26, "Behold the fowls of the air: for they sow not, neither do they reap, nor gather into barns; yet your heavenly Father feeds them," and in Matthew 10:31 you say, "Fear ye not therefore, ye are of more value than many sparrows".

Today I petition by the blood of the Lamb for Your grace and favour of finances in my life, and that You would expand my influence in many ways. Draw and attract destiny helpers to my household and enlarge my borders, and the parameters of the blessings of my household.

You did it for Jabez; now I trust that you will do it for my household. It says in Psalms 149:4, "For the LORD taketh pleasure in His people: He will beautify the meek with salvation."

I acknowledge you as the great door opener and bestower of great blessings of financial wealth, so that I can give to Your work on earth.

You made Abraham wealthy, and you made Solomon wealthy, and you made Job wealthy; therefore, you can make my household wealthy for Your name's sake and for the work of Your ministry. Be our exceeding greatness and joy unspeakable so that my household may be filled with Your glory.

Bestow upon my household today supernatural power to gain wealth and supernatural manifestations of blessings from unexpected places.

Smash through every obstacle, opposition, and resistance that stands in the way of my breakthrough and blessings. I declare in the name of Jesus that my household will see the goodness of the Lord in the land of the living.

No weapon formed against my household shall prosper, and every crooked path shall be straightened now, in Jesus' name!

Lord Jesus, upon the authority of Your word in Exodus 23:25 and Deuteronomy 7:13, **"I stand erect in the spirit and invoke the authoritative capacity of the Kavod glory and the fire of the Shekhinah in my mouth, in my prayers, and around me right now."**

All the wealth of the ungodly, I call you forth into the hands of my household by the verdict and jurisdiction of the Word of God in Proverbs 13:22. With this authority, I curse the demons of financial miscarriage. Let the breath of God breathe upon my family's blessings.

Let the demons of financial infertility, wealth barrenness, poverty, and lack be roasted and destroyed by the sevenfold celestial flames of the presence of the Godhead.
Lord God Almighty, You said in Psalms 2:8, **"Ask of Me, and I shall give you the heathen for your inheritance, and the uttermost parts of the earth for your possession."**

I loose the belly of the heavens and the Earth and command great fountains of wealth to run into my life, and into the life of my children and my children's children.

By the verdict of the Grand Juror of the inner Divine Council of the celestial kingdom of God, and the Lamb who is without blemish, let all people who do not know me pour into my bosom from every tribe, tongue, nation, age, and gender: from the North, South, East, and West, according to Luke 6:38 and Deuteronomy 28:6-12.

I command Proverbs 3:10 to come alive and take effect in my household. Hence, I command by the verdict of the eternal flame of God's presence, which carries the eternal blessings, let my barns be filled with plenty, and thy presses burst out with new wine. Let my oils flow without ceasing, and the provisions to sustain my life and family begin to flow like a mighty rushing river, which never fails, effective immediately.

By authority in Jesus, let the wealth of all categories and financial favours begin to flow into my life and my household. Let the Lord be magnified continually.

Let the gates of wealth swing open, let the walls of barriers be broken down to leveled ground, and let the river of wealth overflow its banks and flow into my household.

Psalms 57:2 says, **"I will cry unto God Most High; unto God that performs all things for me."**

I speak into the atmosphere of the heavens and the earth, and I speak forth Psalms 68:19, **"Blessed be the Lord, who daily loadeth us with benefits, even the God of our salvation."**

SAY THIS WITH FORCE OUT LOUD
> **Lucifer! The Blood of Jesus of Nazareth rebukes you! Release my finances NOW!**
> **NOW! In Jesus name.**

> **Devil! The Blood and Light of Jesus of Nazareth is rebukes you! Release my finances NOW!**
> **NOW! In Jesus name.**

Let the daily benefits from the God of our salvation come upon my household, and may we be loaded daily, in Jesus' name.
It is written in Psalms 37:25, **"I have not seen the righteous forsaken, or his children begging bread".**
Vs. 26, **"All the day long he deals graciously and lends, and his children are blessed."**

Let the benediction of Heaven fall upon my household now, and let my household be blessed with continual blessings daily. Let favour

fall upon my children and let them reap the blessings of my graciousness and kindness towards others.
Let my household come into alignment with the laws of great wealth and family blessings, in Jesus' name.

Heavenly Father, my heart is full of gratitude, thanking You for the financial prosperity and blessings You have showered upon me and my household.
Your abundant provision has brought us stability, comfort, and the ability to thrive. I am deeply grateful for Your generosity and the opportunities You have given us.
Thank you for guiding us in managing our resources wisely and for the financial wisdom that has helped us grow and prosper.
I am thankful for the peace and security that financial stability brings, and for the ability to support and help others through my blessings.

May we continue to honour You with our wealth, using it to make a positive impact in the lives of those around us and to further Your kingdom.
These I pray in the name of Jesus the Messiah of Nazareth, Amen and Amen!

6. SUPERNATURAL FAVOR FOR YOUR HOUSEHOLD

Heavenly Father, in the name of Jesus, I come before You with a humble heart, seeking Your divine favour upon my household. Lord, You are the source of all goodness and mercy.
I petition you for the extraordinary favour of my household, that you would grace and furnish my household with favours beyond comprehension.

Exodus 12:36, ″**And the LORD gave the people favour in the sight of the Egyptians, so that they lent unto them** *such things as they required.* **And they spoiled the Egyptians.**″

I ask that you pour out your supernatural favour upon us, that we may experience grace in every aspect of our lives.

In Luke 12, You say that we should consider the ravens; they neither sow nor reap, they have neither storehouse nor barn, and yet You feed them. How much more valuable are we than the birds!

And if God so clothes the grass of the field, which is alive today and tomorrow is thrown into the oven, how much more will You clothe us! Therefore, we will diligently observe the words of this covenant in order that we may succeed in everything that we do (Deut 29:9).

All the peoples of the earth shall see that we are called by the name of the LORD, and they shall be afraid of us. The LORD will make us abound in prosperity, in the fruit of our womb, in the fruit of our livestock, and in the fruit of our ground in the land that the LORD swore to give us.

The LORD will open for us His rich storehouse, the Heavens, to give the rain of our land in its season and to bless all our undertakings. We will lend to many nations, but we will not borrow. The LORD will make us the head and not the tail; we shall be only at the top and not at the bottom.

According to Deuteronomy 7:20, I ask You, LORD, to send the hornets against those who are hidden under demonic armour and demonic coverings so that they will be exposed, in Jesus Name!

I love the LORD, because He has heard my voice and my supplications. Because He inclined His ear to me, therefore I will call on Him as long as I live. What shall I return to the LORD for all His bounty to me?
I will lift up the Cup of Salvation and call on the Name of the LORD, I will pay my vows to the LORD in the presence of all His people (Psalm 116).

Now, Heavenly Father, I thank You for the countless blessings You have bestowed upon my household.
I am grateful for Your love, grace, and mercy that surround me each day. Thank you for the gift of life, for my family and friends, and for the opportunities you provide. Your provision and protection are beyond measure, and I am humbled by your generosity.

Help me to always remember Your goodness and to express my gratitude in all circumstances. May we use the blessings You have given us to bless others and bring glory to Your name.

Holy Father, by the sceptre of your right hand, and the jurisdiction of your throne of fire, lightning, voices, and thunders, pour down this day supernatural and uncommon favours upon me and my household that will lead us to prosperous destinations.

Let supernatural and uncommon favours bring me and my household before great men, nobles, kings, and princes. And may we find great favour with those in authority, in Jesus' mighty name.

I declare by fire and the word of God that the doors of supernatural and uncommon favours are opening for me and my household in this season and the next, in Jesus' name.

I speak into the heavens and the earth by fire of the Holy Spirit, and I say let the dew of supernatural and uncommon favours rest upon the heads of every member of my household, and let their garments be wet with the great grace of extraordinary proportion, in Jesus' name.

I pray for divine connections that will provoke supernatural and uncommon favours in the paths of me and my household across educational, financial, material, spiritual, social, and economic aspects, in Jesus' name.

Supernatural and uncommon favours for supernatural healing and restoration in my health and body, flow within my home now and fight against all that are destroyers of good things, now, in Jesus' name.

Father, break every barrier and hindrance blocking my favour, and let the rain of your presence bring with it the grace of favour with God and favour with man, now, in Jesus name.

Let Your supernatural and uncommon favours follow me and my household in all dealings, business, and endeavours, and may we find favours where others were rejected, driven out, or killed, in Jesus' name.

Let the walls of my family household be built with stones of favour, and let my household be beautified after the similitude of a palace. Let the tapestry and covering be supernatural and uncommon favours, and let wealth be the pillars of my household, in Jesus' mighty name.

May I find favour in the sight of men, in Jesus' mighty name. (Proverbs 3:4, NIV)

Lord, open doors of wisdom and understanding in my spiritual journey, and let supernatural and uncommon favours, follow me as they followed Abraham, Isaac, and Israel, in Jesus' mighty name.

I ask for supernatural favour come upon me and my household in all applications, interviews, and requests for jobs.

Father, let supernatural and uncommon favours for good and godly marriages and family structure be upon my household.

I pray for supernatural and uncommon favours in the workplace for divine promotion. (Psalm 75:6-70).

Let my favours be accompanied by the four winds of the Earth, and let the glory of favour pursue me and overtake me with all its benefits, in Jesus name.

Father, open doors of supernatural and uncommon favours for me and my household in places I least expect.

Father, let the power of divine grace for the acceleration of supernatural and uncommon favours be upon me and my household, effective immediately.

I command gates of supernatural and uncommon favours to open in the north, south, east, and west for me and my household, in Jesus' name.

In the name of Jesus I say, all dark weight sitting upon my favour, be overthrown by fire now, and release my favour, in Jesus' name.

I decree that the enemies of my favours will see great favours come upon me and be mute and mummified in shame and disgrace, in Jesus' name.

All evil entities of the terrestrial and celestial realms who have purposed in themselves to fight against my favour, shall fight against themselves with their own hands, in Jesus' name.

.
By the hand of ElShaddai, let supernatural and uncommon favours, pursue my household and open doors of creative ideas and innovations in my household. Let businesses be birthed in Jesus' name.

Now Heavenly Father, I thank You for the countless blessings You have bestowed upon my household. I am grateful for Your love, grace, and mercy that surround my household each day. Thank You for the gift of life, for my family and friends, and for the opportunities You provide. Your provision and protection are beyond measure, and I am humbled by Your generosity.

Help my household to always remember Your goodness and to express my gratitude in all circumstances. May I use the blessings You have given to my household to bless others and bring glory to Your name.
In Jesus' name, I pray, Amen and Amen.

7. PRAYER TO INVOKE HOUSEHOLD SUPERNATURAL BLESSINGS

Heavenly, I come to Your presence to humble myself and repent for my sins and iniquities, and those of my ancestors and parents from my mother's house and my father's house, so that the Blood of Christ would remove all allegations against my blessings.

I have seen my blessings being hindered, and I have not been experiencing Your blessings in ways that will confound my adversaries and enemies. Therefore, today through Your Son Jesus of Nazareth, I detest all personal and family transgressions and trespasses, and ask You to remove from me every sin, evil covenant, and iniquity that has given demons astral right to capture my blessings in the Land, Sea, and Air. By the Judicial Council of Your mercy, judgement and compassion, revive the verdict of the judicial Blood of the Lamb and the Mercy Seat, and acquit me of all allegations, accusations, and condemnations, and of all sins, evil, and wickedness embedded in me from my youth till now.

"Let them shout for joy, and be glad, that favour my righteous cause: yea, let them say continually, Let the LORD be magnified, which hath pleasure in the prosperity of his servant." [Psalms 35:27]
According to the words of the Messiah Jesus in Mark 16:17, "And these signs shall follow them that believe; in my name shall they cast out devils."

On this authority, by fire I break the backbone of the spirit of delay in my life, effective immediately.

Lord God, Deuteronomy 28 gives the promise of blessing as we diligently observe all Your commandments, that You will set us high above all the nations of the earth; all these blessings shall come upon us and overtake us, as we obey the LORD our God: Blessed shall we be in the city and blessed shall we be in the field.

Blessed shall be the fruit of our womb, the fruit of our ground, and the fruit of our livestock, both the increase of our cattle and the issue of our flock. Blessed shall be our basket and our kneading bowl. Blessed shall we be when we come in, and blessed shall we be when we go out.
The LORD will cause our enemies who rise against us to be defeated before us; they shall come out against us one way and flee before us seven ways.

The LORD will command His blessing upon us in our barns, and in all that we undertake; He will bless us in the land that the LORD our God is giving us. The LORD will establish us as His holy people, as He has sworn to us, as we keep the commandments of the LORD our God and walk in His ways.

By the verdict of the Council of Mount Zion in the sides of the North, the City of the Great King, I now speak forth, decree, and declare that the season of delay in my life is hereby terminated, effective immediately. I call this wealth out from the hands of the wicked, and out of the hands of my enemies, and command it to be transferred into my hands.

By the authority of Jesus of Nazareth, I created reservoirs to accommodate my blessings of oil, corn, grain, wheat, new wine, milk, and honey.

I declare by fire, all channels of my blessings that have been blocked from my youth till now are henceforth unblocked.
I call upon the power of Jesus to unclog these channels now, in Jesus Name.

Spirit of the Living God, I welcome You to move like a mighty, rushing wind over my life. Release Your breakthrough anointing to flow through me and propel me forward into my promised land. Give me eyes to see the open doors of favour that others are blind to. Fill me with boldness to seize divinely orchestrated opportunities without hesitation.

It is written in Isaiah 25:6, "And in this mountain shall Yahuah Tseva'oth make unto all people a feast of fat things, a feast of wines on the lees, of fat things full of marrow, of wines on the lees well refined."

Blessings that are locked up in my family bloodline, let them begin to gravitate towards me with accelerated velocity now, in Jesus Name.

All good family blessings that are buried with my ancestors, let these blessings be recovered from the great beyond and be transferred to my life now, that I may become the beneficiary of the family wealth, in Jesus name.

In the name of Jesus of Nazareth, I command the heavens and the earth to be reconfigured and reconditioned now, to accommodate, attract, and channel uncommon favours and blessings into my life, from the North, South, East, and West, effective immediately.

The delay of my financial blessings, material blessings, blessings of clothes, food, technology, electronic devices, my home, and furnishings has come to an end, in Jesus name.

All my heavenly blessings confiscated in the cosmic net of the second heaven vibrate at a higher frequency by the fire of Jesus Christ and burn to ashes the powers of hell that are holding you bound in darkness.

In the name of Jesus, the Christ of Nazareth, let the cosmic nets be burned to ash, and release my blessings and all answers to my prayers, effective immediately.

All partition, covering, shelter, barricade, satanic interference, astral manipulation, and wall that are keeping the blessings of God from flowing into my life, let these evil powers explode to pieces now and turn to useless powder, in the mighty name of Jesus.

Every evil beast that has swallowed my blessings, I cut the belly of this demonic beast with the sword of the Holy Spirit and retrieve my blessings by fire and by force.

Accumulated blessings from unknown sources, blessings of enormous proportion locate me and answer all my needs now, in Jesus Name.

Whoever is holding my wealth and finances in their hand, let my success become too heavy to hold any longer, and wherever my finances are being held, let them become like a burning fire coal, too hot for the kingdom of darkness to hold any longer.

I will no longer drink from the cup of poverty and lack, and poverty and lack are not my portion and inheritance; neither am I any longer a beneficiary of poverty.

The womb of my destiny will conceive productivity and success financially. I declare I am a conceiver of success, of great and mighty things, and my paths are successful paths.
Let Money in the North, South, East, and West receive ears and hear my voice as I now say, Money, come forth and manifest in my life. Become my servant and work for me and answer all things that pertain to my needs and wants, now, effective immediately.

Let wealth run after me and find me, even if I am hiding from wealth.

Let wealth surround me like a wealthy garment, and let my days, weeks, months, and years be filled with unexpected accumulation and amounts of wealth, to the glory of God the Father.

Let financial prosperity and the prosperity of favour rain upon me like the dew of Mount Zion and the dew of Mount Hermon, where the Lord has commanded his blessings.

Father, in the name of the Savior Jesus, through prayer, I build barricades and barriers of incomprehensible protection of fire, and permanent walls and defenses of Light around my blessings in the second heaven, or in the hands of the Angels, or wherever my blessings are located within the trajectory leading to my life.

Heavenly Father, in the name of Jesus I petition you for the finances of my household, that you would grace our financial well-being:
- In Luke 12 You say that we should consider the ravens; they neither sow nor reap, they have neither storehouse nor barn, and yet You feed them. How much more valuable are we than the birds!
- And if God so clothes the grass of the field, which is alive today and tomorrow is thrown into the oven, how much more will You clothe us!
- Therefore, we will diligently observe the Words of this Covenant, in order that we may succeed in everything that we do. (Deut 29:9).
- Deuteronomy 28 gives the promise of blessing as we diligently observe all Your Commandments, that You will set us high above all the nations of the earth; all these blessings shall come upon us and overtake us, as we obey the LORD our God: Blessed shall we be in the city and blessed shall we be in the field.

- Blessed shall be the fruit of our womb, the fruit of our ground, and the fruit of our livestock, both the increase of our cattle and the issue of our flock. Blessed shall be our basket and our kneading bowl. Blessed shall we be when we come in, and blessed shall we be when we go out. The LORD will cause our enemies who rise against us to be defeated before us; they shall come out against us one way and flee before us seven ways.
- The LORD will command His blessing upon us in our barns, and in all that we undertake; He will bless us in the land that the LORD our God is giving us. The LORD will establish us as His Holy people, as He has sworn to us, as we keep the commandments of the LORD our God and walk in His ways.
- All the peoples of the earth shall see that we are called by the Name of the LORD, and they shall be afraid of us. The LORD will make us abound in prosperity, in the fruit of our womb, in the fruit of our livestock, and in the fruit of our ground in the land that the LORD swore to give us.
- The LORD will open for us His rich storehouse, the Heavens, to give the rain of our land in its season and to bless all our undertakings. We will lend to many nations, but we will not borrow. The LORD will make us the head, and not the tail; we shall be only at the top, and not at the bottom. According to Deuteronomy 7:20, I ask You LORD to send the hornets against those who are hidden under demonic armour and demonic coverings so that they will be exposed, in Jesus Name!

8. PROTECTION FOR YOUR HOUSEHOLD

Heavenly Father, I come before You today with a heart full of gratitude, acknowledging Your sovereignty and love.

Father, according to your word in Hebrews 4:16, I now come with boldness to your fiery throne of grace, made of sapphire, seeking your holy intervention in the matter of increase protection for family household.

I request today that the Divine Council of the Almighty God, who is the Grand Judge of the Heavens and the Earth, be seated for my sake, and that of my household, and let my cause now be brought before the Lord of all the earth.

God of the Heavens and Earth, I am requesting a divine judicial verdict that a restraining order be released from your eternal Courts, with a mandate that prompt and unwavering cherubic protection be given to my household.

I humbly ask that you release over my entire household the protective celestial duties of your celestial beings. Your word says, you will give your angels charge over us, to keep us and bear us up. Therefore, I request protection from your Cherubim, Seraphim, the great fiery troops of archangels [1 Thessalonians 4:16] the Thrones – [Col 1:16], Dominions – [Col 1:16], Angels – [Rom 8:38], the Might – [Eph 1:21], the four winds of the Earth and the incorporeal special forces of the army of God directed by Michael the archangel [2Kings Chp. 6:16-17.]

Lord, I ask for Your covering over our home, and that linking angels be set around my household.
By your authority through the seven lamps of burning fire of God, deploy pillars of fire and heavenly assistance to assist me and my household, and to enforce resistance against Hell.

May your attention be turned and focussed upon my family household, as your fasten your eyes upon each member thereof. You are our refuge and strength, our protector, and our shield in times of trouble, and in the continual battles of confrontations and contestations.

By your authority, I invoke fire and command by my divine jurisdiction through the Blood of the Lamb that all witchcraft items that have been used, or is being used to conjure, sustain, or reactivate a curse upon my life and household be turn to powder, in Jesus' holy and mighty name.

Lord Jesus, trouble the evil waters that are troubling my home; discomfit them.

Protect my household from demonic invasion, intrusion, and violation. I destroy all demonic portals that seek to open in my home through enchantment, in Jesus' name.

I barricade myself, my home, and household. Wherever any member of my household is, let there be barriers of incomprehensible force, and permanent walls of reinforced resistance and defenses of lightning to protect my household members from assassins sent by the prince of darkness.

Every link or communication device that is set up in my household or is scheduled to be set up in my home, I dismantle its functionality and scatter its molecules by the fire of the Blood of Jesus.

Let my household be protected from the assaults of the esoteric powers, altars, and destructive mechanisms and principles set by the Devil.

Place a hedge of protection around us, guarding us from any harm, danger, or evil influence sent against us through occult vibrations and sound waves for psychic manipulation.
Protect us from arrows of physical threats, accidents, and illness, and the tridents of the tritons, death hunters, and other astral forces pursuing me and my household.

I pray against enchanted blood, urine, faeces, or any other substance that would be thrown on my property as a ritual and means of enchantment.
Let there be a combat of fire, and let holy fire answer the strange fires that are lit against my household.

Neutralize all darts, arrows, artillery, and combat strategies that are used against my household. Let these be met and confronted by fire in midair, on land, and underwater.

Under the law of God's protection, I call into order everything in my household that is out of order, and I align all misalignments in my household that were set by the elemental spirits of the four worlds of the universe.

O Lord Almighty, keep my household safe from natural disasters, accidents of all kinds, and every unforeseen danger that may lurk in secret places, seeking an opportune time to arise.

When the hosts of the heavens, the moon, the sun, and the stars are activated against my household through incantations of witchcraft, reinforce the covering over my household.
We trust in Your ability to keep us safe, knowing that You are our defender, and that no weapon formed against us from beyond the twelve gates of Hell shall prosper.

Father, I pray for Your spiritual protection as well. Guard our hearts and minds from the attacks of the enemy. Protect us from negative influences, from deceit, from fear, and from all psychic elements that are stationed and programmed against my home for its destruction.

Let the evil forces that seek to disrupt our peace catch fire and be consumed by vehement flames from Your throne. Help us to remain strong in faith, to stand firm in Your Word, and to be alert to any lies or temptations that may seek to divide or distract us. May Your truth be a shield that guards our hearts and minds in Christ Jesus.

I pray for Your protection over our finances, Lord. Shield us from financial hardship, fraud, and any situation that could cause stress or worry. Guide us in making wise and prudent decisions and help us to trust in Your provision. May we be good stewards of the resources You have given us, and may You bless our efforts as we seek to honour You in our work, our spending, and our giving.

Father, I ask for Your protection over our health. Keep us safe from the spirit of infirmity, illness, injury, and disease, and the spirit of plague.
Protect our physical well-being and give us the strength and energy we need to fulfill our daily responsibilities. Help us to make healthy choices that honour You and to care for our bodies as temples of Your Holy Spirit.
Keep us from the demonic snares of unhealthy habits and grant us the discipline to live well.

Above all, Lord, I pray for Your presence to fill our home. May Your Spirit dwell with us, bringing comfort, joy, and peace. Where there is fear, replace it with faith; where there is anxiety, replace it with Your perfect peace. Let our home be a sanctuary of love, joy, and protection, a place where Your presence is felt in every corner.

I place my household in Your loving care, trusting that You will protect us from all harm. I ask that You send Your angels to watch over us and to guard our home day and night. May we always feel secure in Your love, and may we rest in the assurance that You are with us, keeping us safe from all dangers.

Thank you, Lord, for Your constant protection and care. Thank You for the gift of family, for the sanctuary of our home, and for Your constant attention over my household.
We trust in You and give You all the glory for the safety and peace that You provide, in Jesus' name, I pray. Amen and Amen!

9. PRAYER FOR SUCCESS IN YOUR HOUSEHOLD

Heavenly Father, I come before You today with a heart full of gratitude and a spirit seeking Your guidance. I thank You for the gift of family, for the love that binds us together, and for the blessings You have already poured into our lives. Lord, You are the source of all good things, and I acknowledge that every success, every opportunity, and every moment of peace comes from Your hand.
I pray an invocation of divine unction for supernatural speed and success to rest upon my household.

I petition the council of Heaven and request that the emerald rainbow would speak into my success and that of my household and activate it hundred-fold.

I ask that You bless the work of our hands, that our efforts may lead to prosperity and complete success. Help us to be diligent and faithful in all that we do, whether in our careers, our studies, or in our roles as spouses, parents, and children. May we work with integrity, wisdom, and perseverance, trusting that You are guiding us every step of the way.

Lord, I ask for success not only in our material endeavors but in the spiritual and emotional well-being of everyone in our home. Grant us success in building strong relationships, founded on love, respect, and understanding.
May we always be quick to listen, slow to speak, and slow to anger. Help us to communicate with kindness and give us the humility to forgive one another when we fall short, so that the forces of the second heaven would not be able to intercept the success of my household.

Father, I ask that You bring peace to my household. Where there is tension, conflict, or stress, I pray for Your seraphic presence to bring calm and resolution. Help us to prioritize each other and the well-being of our family. May we never lose sight of the importance of love, patience, and unity, for these are the true measures of success in our home.

Lord, I also pray for success in our financial endeavours. You are ElShaddai, the God of many breasts, the ultimate provider who provided for Abraham by this name.

I trust in Your ability to meet all our needs. I ask for Your provision to be abundant and for Your wisdom to guide our financial decisions. May we be good stewards of the resources You've entrusted to us, and may our finances reflect Your faithfulness. Give us the discipline to budget wisely, save diligently, and give generously, knowing that success is not just about wealth but about using our resources to bless others and honour You.

I pray for success in our health and well-being. Lord, I ask that You protect each member of my household from illness and harm. Grant us the strength to care for our bodies, to make healthy choices, and to support each other in maintaining our physical, mental, and emotional health. Help us to live in a way that honours You and promotes harmony in my home.

Above all, Father, I pray that the success we experience would glorify You. May everything, we achieve be a reflection of Your love and grace. Help us to never forget that true success is found not in wealth, status, or achievements, but in living according to Your will and being faithful to the calling You have placed on our lives.

This pray I pray in the mighty name of Jesus of Nazareth, Amen and Amen!

10. PRAYERS AGAINST CURSES OF HOUSEHOLD INFIRMITY

Lord our God, King of the ages, All-powerful and All-mighty who sits between the Cherubim of burning coals, You, the Lord of all flesh, You know our frame and remember that we are mortal.

We come boldly unto the throne of grace, that we may obtain mercy and find grace to help in time of need (Heb. 4:16).

We seek help from the golden altar of Heaven through the sacrificial death of the Lamb of God and implore the judicial authority of the wounds of the Lamb who was slain against household infirmity tonight. Have mercy on your people here today according to the multitude of your lovingkindness and your tender mercies. It is written in Isaiah 53:4-5 "Surely he has borne our infirmities and carried our diseases..."

Let our cry for help trigger an emergency alert to accelerate the velocity of mercy for intervention on our behalf. Psalms 70:1 says, "Make haste, O God, to deliver me; make haste to help me, O LORD."

Therefore, we summon a "holy rebuke" from the Court Room and divine Council in Heaven against all spirits of household infirmity that have imprisoned your people and have set themselves upon your people to afflict them through ancient astral rights, legal grounds, and ethereal bridges coming from your ancestral genealogy.

O God, judge and vindicator, who is clothed with fire and light, arise and fight the battles of all those who are here against various household infirmities and the spirit of premature death attached to them. By your pillar of Fire by night and Cloud by day, let the warfront battle wage hotter than blazing and raging fire and release angelic artillery and resistances against the sophisticated weapons of the sting of death, the emperor of death, the agents of death, the bounty hunters, death hunters, and death reapers who seek to take our lives by household infirmity.

Let our cry for help trigger an emergency alert to accelerate the velocity of mercy for intervention on our behalf.

My God and Father, I place the life of all your people here upon the platform of your judicial council. Behold, the Tribunal of the night has ruled against them.

My God and Father, by the blood of Jesus of Nazareth, we invoke the judicial intervention of Heaven to rule against any and every processing, proceeding, and lawsuit in the tribunal of the night that has set in its course against the life of everyone here listening.

"And now, Lord, behold their threatenings: and grant unto thy servants, that with all boldness they may speak thy word," as it is written in Acts 4:29.

By the authority of Jesus Christ and the power of the Holy Spirit of Jesus, we condemn every condemnation laid over your life by the grand juror of the Judicial Court of the kingdom of darkness, by the attorney general of Hell, by the magistrate of esoteric forces, and by the high judge of the Devil's kingdom.

Your word says, O Lord, in Psalms 94:21, "They gather themselves together against the soul of the righteous and condemn the innocent blood." But it is written in Psalms 109:31, "For he shall stand at the right hand of the poor, to save him from those that condemn his soul."

All decisions taken in the Courts of Darkness against your life to destroy your body by household infirmity, let Heaven overrule these evil decisions now.

Every realm and astral plane receiving psychic commands through witchcraft, incantations, sins, and family iniquities to sustain cycles of invasion and manipulation of your health may the terror of God Almighty bring judgment upon these evil powers. Every evil power of the full moon, new moon, waxing moon, waning moon, season, star, planet, weather pattern, and planetary alignment charged with psychic commands from the astral layers to control your infirmity in my household,

Every demon waging war over your body and health. Let God arise and destroy the powers of death and household infirmity.

Effective immediately, by the wounds of the body of Jesus the Messiah of Nazareth, and by the blood and water of His side, we as a household disarm and cancel every impending organ failure, organ disease, or malignant or benign household infirmity that is mandated through psychic commands to rule in your body.

By the name of Jesus Christ, with hot chains of fire and by force, I bring into subjection to the power of Jesus Christ of Nazareth, every imagination and high thing, every judicial platform, demonic judge, satanic juror, evil bailiff, occult attorney, demonic false witnesses, every evil perpetrator, instigator of evil, and every satanic law and order.

Arise to my help, Psalms 121:2, "My help cometh from the LORD, which made heaven and earth."

Let the three that bear witness in earth, the Spirit, the water, and the blood [1 John 5:8] arise against the highest council of darkness and condemn their verdict to destroy us by household infirmity.

Your word says you sent forth your word and healed our diseases; therefore, WE stand erected in the authoritative capacity of the blood, water, and Spirit of Jesus of Nazareth, and by the authority of your word and name, O Yah, we address household infirmity by inheritance, paternal, genealogical, traits, ethnic, racial, family line, bloodline, roots, family tree, ancestral, and hereditary curses that are the result of the sins of the fathers (Jeremiah 32:18), especially witchcraft, occultism, perversion, and idolatry.

We call upon the judicial blood of Jesus to acquit everyone here from these evil allegations, accusations, condemnations, and strongholds by which the spirit of household infirmity has set itself in the body of the people battling household infirmity.

By the Throne of El-Shaddai, and by the authority of the Word of the Almighty, we bind with hot chains of holy fire the spirit of death, the curse of family calamity, and household infirmity by abnormalities in the body.

Psalms 41:2, "The LORD will preserve him and keep him alive; and he shall be blessed upon the earth: and thou wilt not deliver him unto the will of his enemies."

Anything that was placed in my body by ingestion or incision, or entered my soul and body during any trauma or any demonic open door, or an evil dream that has subjected you to become the victim, a prisoner, an object and subject of the demon of household infirmity, and every psychic entity or agent of darkness that has placed a sigil or mark of household infirmity upon my household in order to strike my family with.

Breast cancer
Leukemia
Bowel cancer
Lung cancer
Lym-phoma
Brain tumor
Bladder cancer
Mela-noma
Prostate cancer
Cervical cancer
Colon cancer
rectal cancer
Kidney cancer
Head and neck cancer
Liver cancer
Sar-coma
Bile duct cancer
Bone tumor
Skin cancer
Endometrial cancer
Pancreatic cancer
Myeloma
Esophageal cancer
Appendix cancer

Infirmities of unknown primary origin
Bone cancer, or cancer of the cardiovascular system,

1 Peter 2:24: **"He Himself bore my sins' in His body on the cross, so that we might die to sins and live for righteousness; 'by His wounds you have been healed."**

Let Respiratory, Digestive, Psychological, Circulatory, Lymphatic, Skeletal, Nervous, Integumentary, Endocrine, Urinary, Mental, Dermatological, and Neurological failures be cancelled and condemned in Jesus' name.

I call for the holy fire of Yah, and the blood of the Lamb of God that was sprinkled upon the mercy seat to intervene and erase every mark, trace, and presence of cancer that was placed in any part of my body by demonic spirits and genetic inheritance.

Psalms 103:2, **"Bless the LORD, O my soul, and forget not all His benefits:"**
Psalms 103:3, **"Who forgiveth all thine iniquities, who healeth all thy diseases;"**
Psalms 103:4, **"Who redeemeth thy life from destruction."**

Send your angels, O Lord, to recover the health and organs of these my people from darkness. Psalms 103:20, **"Bless the LORD, ye his angels, that excel in strength"**.

By the power of the Holy Spirit of Jesus, I revoke all witchcraft incantations done over my body, and I destroy any witchcraft hex and cage that are over my health, and I retrieve by fire my health and organs from the Gates of Hell; I smash to pieces every pendant,

cauldron, black box, vase, bottle, or any other vessel in which my health is trapped.
health challenges, including infectious diseases, non-communicable diseases, and injuries, infectious diseases, including HIV/AIDS, tuberculosis, pneumonia, dengue, and diarrhoea, ·noncommunicable diseases and Infectious diseases.

Your word says in Exodus 23:25, **"You shall serve the Lord your God, and He will bless your bread and your water, and I will take sickness away from among you."**

Jeremiah 17:14 says, **"Heal me, O LORD, and I shall be healed; save me, and I shall be saved: for thou art my praise."**

Jeremiah 30:17 says, **"For I will restore health unto thee, and I will heal thee of thy wounds, saith the LORD."**

Isaiah 53:5 says, **"But he was wounded for my transgressions, he was bruised for my iniquities; the chastisement of my peace was laid upon him, and by his wounds we are healed."**

Matthew 10:1 says, **"Jesus called his twelve disciples to him and gave them authority to drive out impure spirits and to heal every disease and sickness."**

Mark 5:34 says, **"He said to her, 'Daughter, your faith has healed you. Go in peace and be freed from your suffering."**
3 John 1:2 says, **"I pray that you may be in good health and prosper."**
3 John 1:2, **"I pray that you may be in good health and prosper."**

11. DESTROYING CURSES SENT INTO YOUR HOUSEHOLD

Heavenly Father, by the jurisdiction of the Spirit, the Water, and the Blood (1 John 5:8), I come to Your judicial platform to implore Your holy intervention.

Because of the evil systems, curses, and strongholds that are haunting my household, I am requesting that your Divine Judicial Council be seated to attend to the case of my household. I hereby petition you, O Adonai, that my household would fall under the verdict of your Mercy Seat and Throne of Grace, and that all things be ruled in our favour.

Lord Jesus, I am made aware by your mercy of the many curses that are corrupting my household due to ancestral and household transgressions.

It is your will that we dwell in the peace and liberty of Christ and be free from all curses and afflictions.

Today, I rise by fire and by faith and declare a holy revolt against all curses plaguing my family household.

I loose my household from every witchcraft chain, lockdown, condemnation, and shutdown, and I destroy and shatter every witchcraft padlock by the power of the lightnings that proceed from the throne of God, for it is written in Revelation 4:5, **"And out of the throne proceeded lightnings and thunderings and voices"**.

By the fire of the light of God's glory, I stand at the intersection between the heavens and the earth, and I bind every curse and malediction that is sitting upon my household.

I address by fire all powers operating within the cosmic ocean, sea, and layers of psychic planes to sustain ancestral curses, personal curses, witchcraft curses, and spoken curses in my household.

Curses of Hell, I revolt against you today, and by the fire and the incense of the holy Altar of Prayer, in the name of Jesus, I nullify, liquidate, and render powerless and impotent your effect and jurisdiction to affect my household any longer.

In the name of Yahusha HaMashiach, I destroy and banish the following curses: insufficient household income, domestic violence, a dysfunctional family, fear, anger, anxiety, and sadness. Also, job loss, economic hardship, divorce, separation, incarceration, illegitimate pregnancy, sexual abuse, physical abuse, infidelity, substance abuse, foreclosure, medical issues, and emergencies.
Let these curses that are haunting and frustrating my household now be broken and their effects nullified, effective immediately, in the name of Jesus of Nazareth.

Every curse sent upon my household to cause mental health problems, disabilities, or illness that would render any member of my family impotent, immobile, or maimed, I curse this curse, in the name of Jesus of Nazareth, and I loose my household from the jurisdiction of this curse.

Every curse laid upon my household because of a parent or relative having alcohol or drug problems, let fire descend from the holy altar of God, and burn out the altar of alcoholism, its priest, and all demons of alcohol. This is a command in the name of Jesus the Nazarene.

By the power of the Holy Spirit, in the name of Jesus and by the fire and the incense of the holy Altar of Prayer, I destroy every curse responsible for family instability, unrest, disruption, disturbances, emotional and mental unsettlement, sadness, gloom, and doom in my household. I nullify, liquidate, and render powerless and impotent their effect and jurisdiction to affect my household any longer.

By the authority of Jesus Christ, I break by lightning and thunder every curse of mental disturbance, emotional disruption, character manipulation, gross calamity, and pestilence.

In the Name of Yahushua HaMashiach of Nazareth, I break every curse in my household that has trapped the members of my family in the lands of darkness, in the shadows of death, in astral labyrinths, within spiritual witchcraft mazes.

Every curse that is currently eating up the joy, peace, prosperity, productivity, success, destiny, future, and well-being of my household, let these curses break now, and all psychic elements and poison be subjected to the judgement of the seven flames of fire, which burn before the Altar of Jesus Christ.

By the power of Jesus Christ, who is exalted above all, I break and banish from my household all curses placed by forest spirits, desert spirits, water spirits, air spirits, subterranean spirits, and other forces of the kingdom of darkness for the dismantling of the peace, unity, and family bond of my household, in the name of Yahusha HaMashiach.

I break, destroy, and nullify all curses of vicious psychic attacks, witchcraft manipulations, swift and progressive destruction, persistent predicaments, recurring calamities, repetitive failures, blockages, hindrances, disappointments, contamination, sensual defilement, marriage dismantlement, disgrace, afflictions, shame, and disgrace, in the name of Yahusha HaMashiach.

I also break, destroy, and nullify from my household all vicious curses of identity fragmentation, mental fragmentation, emotional fragmentation, multiple personality disorder, dissociative identity disorder, forgetfulness, memory loss, mental confusion, and backwardness that are currently sitting in my household.

In the name of Yahusha HaMashiach, I nullify, liquidate, and render powerless and impotent all demonic effects and jurisdiction to affect my household.
I dismantle all curses that carry the mandate for death, annihilation, madness, and destruction of the joy, peace, finances, health, and success of my household.
Therefore, I claim freedom for my household, and I destroy and banish from my family home all curses of character configuration and de-characterization that resemble and represent the character of demonic snakes, newts, salamanders, spiders, vipers, dragons, and beasts in the name of Jesus of Nazareth.

Every curse that causes the light of my household to turn to darkness, break now and be dismantled by the fire of Seraphim and the holy altar of Yah. For it is written, let your light shine, in the name of Yahusha HaMashiach.

Whatever hole in the ground my household was placed in by witchcraft, I pray and command the life of my family household to be restored by the fire of the Holy Spirit of Jesus Christ.

I call upon the Voice of the Lord in Psalms 29:3 to neutralize, disarm, and dismantle the force of these water occult powers and psychic manipulations in the name of Yahusha HaMashiach.

Let all angelic and demonic seeds, planted in my household during the nocturnal and diurnal gates, be destroyed by the power of the unity of the Spirit, the Blood, and the Water of Christ, in Jesus' name.

Let every curse over my household that is most active and vibrant within the twilight zone and the gate of the dawn be broken, effective immediately, in the name of Yahusha HaMashiach.

In the name of Yahusha HaMashiach, I renounce, nullify, and banish every blood covenant and witchcraft alliance with the kingdom of darkness that was made with my family household, physically or spiritually, consciously or unconsciously, directly or indirectly.

Father, in the Name of Jesus of Nazareth, I renounce any witchcraft concoction given to me in a dream, and I renounce any and every foul spirit placed in my body as spirit guides, watchers, and tormentors.

Whatever hole in the ground my life was placed in by witchcraft, I pray and command that my life be restored to me by the fire of the Holy Spirit of Jesus Christ.

All demonic rodents and land creatures, foul birds, monkeys, octopus spirits, leeches, and other mysterious creatures from the water, forest, desert, and underground kingdom of Hell, haunting, constricting, tormenting, and afflicting my household, let fire descend from the seven altars of God and burn you demons to dry powder, in the name of Yahusha HaMashiach.

Every demon behind these curses, I place chains of holy fire upon their hands and feet, and I send them into exile to be crushed under the feet of higher beasts, in the name of Yahusha HaMashiach.

Thank you for delivering my household from curses. Allow my household to be sealed unto the day of redemption, according to Ephesians 4:30, and keep me in the will of Your Holy Spirit, now and forever, world without end.

I pray for all these things in the powerful and matchless name of Jesus Christ. Amen and Amen!

12. PRAYERS AGAINST SPIRITS THAT FRUSTRATES HOUSEHOLDS

Heavenly Father, you are Abba, the Aleph-Bet.
I come before You today, seeking the flourishing of Your love, healing, deliverance, and presence against all that frustrates my household and its purposes.

I pray that all things the devil is using as a point of reference to frustrate my household.
I pray that anything that has entered my household, which the enemy is using as a ground to debate my household's blessings, peace, and prosperity, let the presence of God render a verdict in favour of my household.

Father, I pray against every spirit causing relationship barriers, bitterness, hatred, resentment, avoidance, repelling communications, withdrawal, low self-esteem, unforgiveness, and emotional and behavioral oppression because of a new stepparent, stepbrother, or stepsister; I break the backbone of this spirit of discord, rejection, and unacceptance in Jesus' name.

I dislodge every root demon and banish these uneasy, discomforting and frustrating spirits from my household, effective immediately, in Jesus' name. According to Psalms 133:1, the brethren of my household shall dwell together in unity, by a divine restraining order, in Jesus' name.
Hence, I invoke the oil of gladness and the oil of joy upon my household [Psalms 45:7, Isaiah 61:3], and I pray for the distribution of the spirit of righteousness to destroy the essence of the spirit of wickedness, that would seek to enter my household to frustrate it.

I pray against every demon using the gate of an adopted member of my household to instil curses and patterns of relationship barriers and other emotional and behavioral oppression. Let these demons be banished from my household now, effective immediately.

Every curse of relationship barriers, bitterness, hatred, resentment, avoidance, repelling communications, withdrawal, low self-esteem, bitterness, unforgiveness, emotional and behavioral oppression that is sitting upon my family household, because of the trauma of domestic violence in the family's foundation, let these spirits be banished from my family home, and every pattern and recurring curse be broken, nullified, and banished from my household now, effective immediately.

Every curse of different personalities clashing in disagreements over ways of doing things, causing discord and hostility, reviling and verbal abuse in the family, I break this curse in the name of Jesus of Nazareth.

I address by fire all powers operating within the cosmic ocean, sea and layers of psychic planes, which are working against my household with weapons of mental disturbances, emotional disruptions and character manipulations, and the absence of Childproofing, every spirit of negligence that would create factors of endangerment and snares of bodily harm.

- **Breaking The Curse Of Household Unemployment**

I come before You with a heart full of faith, knowing that You are my Provider and the One who opens doors that no man can shut. I lift up every member of my household, especially those facing unemployment or financial challenges, asking for Your divine intervention.

Lord, it is written in Psalms 34:10, **"The young lions do lack, and suffer hunger: But they that seek the LORD shall not want any good thing."**

Father, it is your will to provide for my household. You said in Deuteronomy 28:12, **"The LORD shall open to you His good treasure, the heaven to give the rain to your land in its season, and to bless all the work of your hand. And you shall loan to many nations, and you shall not borrow."**

Every curse of unemployment sitting upon my family household, subduing my household to demonic curses of ridicule, shame, disgrace, relationship barriers, bitterness, resentment, avoidance, repelling communications, withdrawal, low self-esteem, bitterness, envy, emotional and behavioral oppression, I break these curses and their effects from over my household. I break and banish from my family every pattern of unemployment and reoccurring rejections in good employment or business opportunities.

Father, by the authority of Jesus of Nazareth, I break every pattern of joblessness, and I command the curse of unemployment to be broken, nullified and banished from my household now, effective immediately.

Father, in the name of Jesus, I break every spirit of stagnation and delay that has held back the employment and opportunities meant for this household. I declare that every barrier to progress is broken now, and the doors of opportunity are opening wide. Your Word says that You have a plan for us, a plan to prosper us and not to harm us, to give us a future and a hope. I stand on that promise today.
I bind the spirit of lack, poverty, and hopelessness. I command these spirits to flee from this home.

Father, I plead for the intervention of the blood of Jesus in the courts of heaven to rule in favour of every job application, interview, and opportunity, that they would be favoured, and Your divine hand would guide every step taken toward employment. Therefore, I say, in the name of Jesus of Nazareth, I banish by fire any spirit that is

sitting upon the resume' of any member of my household, or hiding the resume,' so that it will be unnoticeable to the employer.
Let fire descend upon this resume; and expose it and its content, in the favour of my household.

Also, I pray, every spirit from the occult kingdoms frustrating the decision of the human resource manager or employer to employ any member of my household after a job interview, I uproot this spirit, and cast it into the crevices of the desert, to become food for the jackals and wild beasts, now [Psalms 63:10].
Therefore,

Lord, I ask You to release wisdom, favour, and creativity into this home. Let every family member who is seeking employment be guided by Your Spirit, and may they be positioned in the right place at the right time. Let divine connections and appointments come forth in unexpected and supernatural ways.
I cancel every word of discouragement and negativity spoken over this home. I declare prosperity, abundance, and fruitful labour in this home. I claim Your provision and Your promises over every financial need. Let Your blessings flow into this household, not only in jobs but in every area of our lives.

I declare that the spirit of diligence will arise, that every individual in this household will be diligent, hardworking, and committed to their calling. May they not grow weary in well-doing, for in due season, they will reap the harvest of their labour.

Father, thank You for the breakthrough that is coming, for Your timely provision, and for the jobs that will be offered. We will rejoice in Your goodness and declare Your faithfulness in all things. In the name of Jesus, we pray and believe. Amen.

Every curse of relationship barrier, bitterness, hatred, resentment, avoidance, repelling communications, withdrawal, low self-esteem, bitterness, emotional depression, financial strains and behavioral oppression, that are sitting upon my family household because of unemployment, let these curses be broken and let these spirits be banished from my home; let every pattern and reoccurring curse of job calamity be broken, nullified and banished from my household, effective immediately.

I break this curse of Parental arguments and violence, that is causing relationship barriers, bitterness, hatred, resentment, avoidance, repelling communications, withdrawal, low self-esteem, bitterness, unforgiveness, emotional and behavioral oppression.
Let all demons of Parental arguments and violence be banished from my household right now, in the name of Jesus of Nazareth.

In the name of Jesus of Nazareth, I break the curse of Jealousy or fighting between brothers and sisters, or among members of the household because of job description, relationship status, appearances, financial status, spiritual beliefs. It is written, in Psalms 133:1, **"Behold, how good and how pleasant it is for brethren to dwell together in unity!"**

13. PRAYER AGAINST DIVORCE IN YOUR HOUSEHOLD

Heavenly Father, I come before You in the name of Jesus, recognizing Your supreme power and authority over all things. You are the Creator of the heavens and the earth, and there is no power greater than Yours. I thank You for Your love, protection, and faithfulness toward me and my family.

Right now, I stand in the gap for my household, and I invoke warfare of fire against the demon of the four elements who is sustaining the curses of divorce and maneuvers of psychic manipulation for marital destruction within my household.

I invoke the divine intervention of the fire of your holy altar to fight against the forces of the aramau astral poison and dismantle the combined elements of astral spirits capable of sustaining daily psychic attacks against members of my household for cycles of one thousand and ninety-five days.

I come against every form of witchcraft, astral bands, psychic manipulation, and psychic attack, and all psychic forces from the seven kingdoms of darkness that have been programmed and stationed in place to destroy my household by division and eventual divorce.

Let the heavens be moved and the clouds gather together to fight against all witchcraft that is done in the air against my household and their marriages.

I break this curse of divorce or separation that is fighting my household, seeking to subject it to ruin, shame, and embarrassment.

Every agent of darkness that has replaced the marital garment of any member of my household with a garment of divorce, marital dysfunction, marital shame and disgrace, marital abuse, and humiliation, etc.

In the mighty name of Jesus Christ, by the fire of the holy altar of prayer, I break every curse, hex, spell, and evil enchantment that has been cast to destroy marital unions in my household within the next four generations.

I call upon the fire of the throne of the Almighty from which proceed lightnings and thunderings and voices; and I pray that the fire of the seven lamps burning before the throne, which are the seven Spirits of God [Rev 4:5], will now descend and destroy to ashes these garments of divorce or separation, in the name of Jesus, the Christ of Nazareth.

Every fake beauty given to my household by the Sirens, Demons, and witches of the kingdom of darkness through the psychic elemental spirits, to cause the spouses in my family to lose taste in their mate because of being unattractive to the eyes, lust toward another person, or dullness in erotic feelings or feelings of indifference, I break these demonic symptoms, curses, and manipulations right now in Jesus' name.
According to what is written in Psalms 139:14, we are fearfully and wonderfully made, and the works of God are marvellous.

I tear off from the members of my household every marital garment of unattractive, unappealing, unattractiveness, unlikeable, disgust, repulsion, revulsion, distaste, contempt, abhorrence, dullness, unbeauteous, uninviting that is causing one spouse to be unappealing to the other.

I release my household from this evil bondage of psychic manipulation, as I declare the war of seraphic fire to intervene and combat every evil within the boundaries of my home.

I cast out and banish all your evil powers and familiar spirits and send you into oblivion, as I restore to my household its true beauty, as the spouses are restored in the name of Jesus.

Let all demons of marital arguments and violence be banished from my household right now, in the name of Jesus of Nazareth.

I break down relationship barriers, bitterness, hatred, resentment, avoidance, repelling communications, withdrawal, unforgiveness, and emotional and behavioral oppression that stand between the spouses in my household.

I storm the kingdom of darkness with flames of destruction, and by fire and lightning demolish every structure of divorce, neutralize all venoms of divorce, consume any existing or upcoming arrow of divorce that has been working against my household through the law of meta-homogeneity, and other forces of Mephistophelian seals of the occult.

I invoke rains of fire, terror, tempest, fiery hails upon the demon Asmodeus, every spirit wife and spirit husband, and elemental spirits working through the law of curses to cause patterns of divorce in my household because of existing and activated evil embargos, demonic links, astral rights, ancestral relationships with occult entities, alliances, agreements with demons by words, blood spill, handwriting, signature, ancestral truce, and evil covenants, ties, and contracts made with the queen of heaven, the queen of the waters, spirits of forest nymphs, water nymphs, sirens, mermaids, spirit of huldra, leshy, the moss folks, wood wives, succubi and incubi, ancestral totem, and every other psychic and elemental power of the forest, land, sea, air, desert, cemetery, and underground.

I nullify and condemn all astral and legal rights, covenants, and links by the Blood of Jesus. I set my home free from all witchcraft and demonic presence in the exalted name of Jesus of Nazareth.

Any evil altar that has formed a mutual relationship between the entities of the occult world and my household, fighting to ambush and lay legal claim to the marriages of my household unto four generations, in order to wreck these marriages in divorce, I banish the influence of these demons and break any curse of Asmodeus, spirit wife, or spirit husband, effective immediately.

Father, I renounce every evil altar, spirit, or person that has spoken or performed acts of witchcraft against my marriage. I command every demonic force sent to sow seeds of division, confusion, anger, bitterness, and unforgiveness to leave my home now, in Jesus' name! I break every chain, every spiritual barrier, and every work of darkness designed to separate spouses within my household.

Lord, I am convinced that marriage that is under Your will and blessings is beautiful and sacred. Marriage with the presence of God, can turn plain water into sweet wine. I am willing to bring the marriage and family of the world to the presence of God and pray that You rule and reign over each family, so Your will be done in our home, the marriage will be happy, and the family blessed.

Keep the bonds in my family's marriages strong and our hearts united. Protect us from misunderstandings, bitterness, and division. Help us to communicate with love, patience, and understanding, so that the enemy cannot sow discord among us. Where there is hurt or conflict, bring healing and reconciliation. May our home be a place where love and peace flourish, and where we always seek to build each other up.

Let Your angels surround us with wings of fire and the wind of Your presence, and may Your presence fill my household with the songs of peace, joy, and unity and with the oil thereof. I declare that no diabolical weapon formed against my household from beneath the waters of the seas and oceans, from beneath the burial grounds, and from behind the curtains of the occult barriers between worlds shall prosper, and every curse of divorce is broken by the power of the cross.

I declare in the name of Jesus, the enemy has nothing, no power no status in our marriage and family. In the name of Jesus, we tear down the wall visible or invisible that is separating the husband and wife; we forsake any indifference, envy, and argument, I break every chains and bondage, remove all the control and obstacles, heal all the harms of our bodies, souls and spirit, restore the health of the family, our soul prosper, open the eyes of our hearts, to understand the ethics of the family of Christ, husband and wife be willing to commit to each other and rebuild the relationship like their first love, with the fear of the Lord, to love and submit to each other,

It is written, "As for me and my household, we will serve the Lord".
I speak healing into our relationship, restoration into our hearts, and renewed love and commitment to one another.
May Your Holy Spirit empower us to forgive and to love, and to walk in unity with each other. We choose to reject any demonic influence, demonic pop-ups, demonic tags, and demonic sigils that seek to destroy marital unions within my household.

Father, cleanse our hearts, our minds, and our home from any evil contamination, demonic deposits, and uncleanness from demonic defilement.
I ask that You uproot all seeds of strife and discord that have been sown by the elemental spirits: the Undines, Sylphs, Salamanders, and Gnomes, and replace them with peace, understanding, and harmony by the presence of your glory.

Let Your will be done in our lives, and may our marriage reflect Your glory.

In the mighty name of Jesus Christ, I declare my household free from every curse, spell, and witchcraft influence. We are covered by the blood of the Lamb, and no evil shall have dominion over us.

I decree that love shall endure in my household by the fire of the incense of the garment of Christ.

14. ANSWER AND RESTORE MY HOUSEHOLD GLORY BY FIRE

Heavenly Father, God of graces and favour. You sit upon the throne of fire and dwell between the cherubim of burning coals, surrounded by righteousness and justice. You are the king of the heavens and the Earth, and all dimensions bow before Your majesty and sovereignty. I come to your holy courts, requesting that you pour the essence and light of your glory upon my household and restore all glories that have been lost, suddenly or over time.

Oh Lord, Your secret place is a place by You [Exo 33:21]. Let Your inner sanctum, holiness, and fire answer my household by fire, and bring my household into Your Inner Chamber of light and glory.
Sanctify my household in the Inner Chambers of your sanctuary, and let holiness be our holy garment.

In this dimension, let your glory restore all glories that the enemy has taken away or caused to depart, and let your light overshadow my household, for your holy shadow is made of splendor, fire, and light.
Lord, restore unto me and my household the glory that we once had, and that which was sent to us which we did not receive.
Let the mysteries of Fire and Godliness dwell upon my household, for Your glory and honour.
Let the presence of Your Holiness, the throne of Your fire and judgement rule in favour of my household, for restoration of our household and family glory.

Allow us to dwell under the presence of your glory, so my household can be as little cubs under your shadow.
Restore to us the glory that people once saw and marvelled.
Restore to us the glory that made us beautiful in the sight of God and man.

Restore to us the glory of favour with God and man, and the honour that once caused men to fall before us in respect.
Give us the presence of your glory, so that we can reflect who you are in your majesty and awe.
Shed light of fire upon my household, O Lord our God, and refine us by the fire of your feet of burnished bronze.

I pray today, restore the glory of my household, and light the fire of a perfect relationship with Your holy Son, Jesus, in our hearts again.
Restore the glory of prayer and travail, the glory of intercession and supplication to my household.

Let your glory fall on us as I petition your divine council to configure and condition my household for your glory to become eminent in our lives. Exodus 33:21, "So *he said to Moses, come. And the LORD said, Behold, there is a place by me, and thou shalt stand upon a rock."*
 Give and restore to my household the Beauty of Holiness and essence of your Shekhinah, by which the brilliance of your love and mercy would emanate from our earthly being.

O Lord, have mercy upon my household, and favour us above our enemies. They have set themselves to cast us down, but Father, we trust in you, for we shall not be put to shame.

Remove the shame and disgrace of my household and render all negative remarks and imaginations futile and useless.
Turn the reproach of my household into honour, praise, and favour with man, and let my enemies see your favour being bestowed upon my household in great measures.

Remove the stigma of blight, humiliation, and public embarrassment from my entire household, from the youngest to the oldest.
Where the public has put their tongues at us in mockery, vindicate us and turn our sorrows into joy, our mourning into laughter, and our tears into great rejoicing.

Restore my household its life, success, business idea, godly desires, expectations, endeavours, destinies, bright future,
Let there be a restoration of godly children, generational blessings, wealth, health, sound minds, virtues, talents, gifts, holy character, potential, successful marriages, money, intellectual capacities, intelligence, moral values, self-worth, integrity, knowledge, and the glory of love, in Jesus' holy name.

By your testimonies, give us many testimonies of your goodness by Your holiness. It is written in Psalm 93:5, "Thy *testimonies are very sure: holiness becometh thine house, O LORD, for ever"*.

Surround my household today, I pray, with the glory of holiness which radiates many colours. Restore unto us the joy of your salvation and renew a right spirit within every one of the members of my household. This I pray in the holiness of your great name.

Lord, You are able to bring beauty and order where there has been chaos and brokenness. I ask that You restore the glory of my household, that it may once again reflect Your goodness, peace, and love.
Father, I pray for Your divine presence to fill every room in my home, cleansing it from any negative influence and renewing it as a place of Your grace and glory. Let Your peace reign in our hearts and in every corner of our dwelling. Bring healing where there has been pain, understanding where there has been division, and love where there has been strife.
Lord, I ask for a fresh outpouring of Your Holy Spirit upon my household.
Let Your wisdom guard our every decision, and Your love strengthen our household relationships. Restore unity among all who live here and help us to honour and respect one another as You have called us to, in Jesus mighty name.

- **Clothing Your Household With The Garment Of Praise**

Every power from the realm of the kingdom of darkness that has replaced my household's garment of praise with a demon of heaviness, I call this replacement or exchange into order, and I say, you demon who has done this, destruction and chains of unbearable torment be upon you now, effective immediately.

I tear off any garment of heaviness placed upon my household, and I call upon the Holy Spirit to place the garment of praise upon us, for it is written in Psalms 107:8, **"Oh that men would praise the LORD for His goodness, and for His wonderful works to the children of men!"**

Let praise continually be in our mouth [Psalms 34:1]. My Lord and God, unite our hearts to fear your name according to Psalms 86:11.

Praises waits for you Lord in my household, for it is written Psalms 65:1, **"Praise waits for You, O God, in Zion; and to You shall the vow be performed."**

Pour the anointing and power of praise upon me and my household, for it is written in Psalms 5:11, **"But let all those that put their trust in you rejoice: let them ever shout for joy, because you defend them: let them also that love your name be joyful in you."**

Psalms 32:11 says, **"Be glad in the LORD and rejoice, you righteous; and shout for joy, all you upright in heart."**

Your word also says in Psalms 35:27, **"Let them shout for joy, and be glad, that favour my righteous cause: yea, let them say continually, Let the LORD be magnified, which hath pleasure in the prosperity of his servant."**

Let praise become a lifestyle and character in my home, and let it never depart, but become a generational garment upon my generation, in the name of Jesus I pray Amen.

- **Oil Of Joy And Beauty Of The Household**

Lord God, You are the God of joy, and your Holy Spirit gives to all who request of your presence. I petition you to lubricate my household with the oil of joy unspeakable.

It is written in Isaiah 61:3, **"To appoint unto them that mourn in Zion, to give unto them beauty for ashes, the oil of joy for mourning, the garment of praise for the spirit of heaviness; that they might be called trees of righteousness, the planting of the LORD, that he might be glorified."**

By the jurisdiction of the golden altar and the mercy seat, my household is called a tree of righteousness and the planting of the Lord (Isaiah 61:3); therefore, the joy that comes from the presence of the Lord is hereby declared the portion of my household, effective immediately.

All you demons who came to rob me and my household of the joy of Jesus, I say by fire, let destruction and chains of unbearable torment, and incomprehensible heat by the coals of the holy altar in Heaven be upon you now, effective immediately.

O Lord of glory and power, give my household the gift of the shout of joy according to Ezekiel 3:13.
Give my household the fullness of joy and pleasures forevermore, according to Psalms 16:11.

Give my household a tabernacle for the sacrifices of joy, according to Psalms 27:6.
Fill my household with the voice of joy and praise, according to Psalms 42:4.
Make me full of joy with thy countenance, according to Acts 2:28.
Give my family household the oil of joy in the place of mourning, according to Isaiah 61:3.

Lord Jesus, Commander in Chief of the Armies of Heaven. Decode the mysteries of joy and unlock its power in my household. Let all benefits that are locked up in the spirit of joy descend like the dew upon my household today and every morning, in the name of Jesus of Nazareth.

I declare that Joy is the portion of my household. We have joy unspeakable and full of glory according to [1Peter 1:8].
My household is dwelling in the secret place of the Most High, and we are abiding under the shadow of the Almighty in the presence of the Lord my Savior [Psalms 91:1]; therefore, my household is receiving the fullness of joy, for it is written in Psalms 16:11: **"In thy presence *is* fullness of joy; at thy right hand *there are* pleasures for evermore."**

Oil of joy, come upon my household now in great measures, in Jesus' name.
I speak into the glory of God through the blood of the holy Oblation of Christ, and I say, joy unspeakable and full of glory, come down in my home and fill my household in great measures and with great pleasures.

Oil of joy from the Holy Spirit, dispel all sadness, disappointment, discouragement, and gloominess from life and that of my household, and fill my home with the oil of everlasting joy.

I decree that the spirit of the fullness of joy shall flow throughout my home like a mighty stream and attract the attention of my neighbours, friends, and foes, in Jesus' name, for it is written in Jeremiah 33:9, **"And it shall be to me a name of joy, a praise and an honour before all the nations of the earth, which shall hear all the good that I do unto them: and they shall fear and tremble for all the goodness and for all the prosperity that I procure unto it.** Enemies of my joy, and the joy of my household, are now removed from my life by force, and are confounded in shame and disgrace.

Every power from the realm of the kingdom of darkness that has replaced the garment of beauty of my household with ashes and has replaced our oil of joy with a spirit of mourning, I call this replacement (or exchange) into order and undo this evil operation.

This I pray, decree, and command in the name of Jesus of Nazareth.

- **Household Ministry**

Father, every power from the realm of the kingdom of darkness that has replaced my household's garment of ministry, causing us to be an unfaithful, incompetent household, and worthless servants as in Your parables, I rebuke these evil powers in Jesus' name.

Lord, I ask for Your divine power to strengthen and empower my household for ministerial work.
Fill all members of my home with Your Holy Spirit to do tasks that are divinely ordained.

I reclaim by fire the ministerial garments for my household, and I command the kingdom of darkness in all realms and spheres to release our ministerial garment that was replaced or exchanged, effective immediately.

Give ministerial wisdom to us that we may speak Your truth with boldness, love, and clarity. Grant my household wisdom to rightly divide the Word of truth and to speak in a way that touches hearts and transforms lives. May Your Word shine from every member of my household and be a light to those who are in darkness, and a source of strength for those who are weary. I surrender the abilities of my household and ask that coals of fire from Your altar be poured upon my household for empowerment and anointing, so that great tasks and divine mandates can be carried out in Your name.

Without You, I can do nothing, but with You, all things are possible. Give my household the empowerment to do Your will and pour the spirit of excellence and faithfulness upon every member of my home. Lord, neutralize the powers of darkness in all realms and dimensions, and disarm their tactic of skilfully maneuvering astral poisons of distraction and attacks against my household.
May my life reflect the love, grace, and power of Christ in a ministerial way, so that others may be drawn closer to You. Thank you for Your Spirit of grace and faith in the work of God, in the name of Jesus of Nazareth, amen.

15. PRAYERS AGAINST HOUSING PROBLEMS

Heavenly Father, I come before Your sovereignty today, humbly requesting angelic intervention from the highest order of the sanctum of Your holiness of fire, in order to dismantle the strongest verdict and velocity of the astral and metaphysical forces that operate at the highest Astro-metaphysical acceleration against my household.

You have given Angels as custodians of the Saints, for Jacob said in Genesis 48:16, **"The Angel who has redeemed me from all evil, bless the lads."**

The regime of the occult forces of the terrestrial and astral realms is seeking to render my household useless and unproductive, seeking to corrupt and poison the atmosphere of my household with the venom of discouragement, overwhelm, weariness, and uncertainty, feelings of inadequacy, and stress. But, Lord, we also know that You are with us, providing comfort, wisdom, and peace beyond understanding. For it is written in Psalms 9:9, **"The LORD also will be a refuge for the oppressed, a refuge in times of trouble."**
It also says in 1 Kings 19:7, **"And the angel of the LORD came again the second time, and touched him, and said, Arise and eat; because the journey is too great for thee."**

Father, it is evident that you are an ever-present help in times of trouble, but behold, O Lord, the 12 gates of hell have been prevailing in specified areas of my household, as the seven astral kingdoms of darkness are programmed to deconfigure and disfigure my household with perpetual problems.

Therefore, by the authority of your word in **Matthew 10:8** where you say, **"Heal *the* sick. Cleanse *the* lepers. Raise *the* dead. Cast out demons."**, and by the power given to me in Mark 16:17-18 where you say, **"And these signs shall follow them that believe; In my name** shall they cast out devils; they shall speak with new tongues; They shall take up serpents;"** I now dismantle the operations of black witchcraft and demonic manipulations in my household, where the snares of perpetual troubles have been programmed to become the daily troubles of my family members.

By the power of fire and the light of the Holy Spirit, in the name of Jesus of Nazareth, I neutralize and banish from my household every demon and occult agent who is lurking and working, seeking to manipulate and alter the moral family structure of my household via occult sound vibrations, using the enigma of the four elements: water, fire, earth, and air.

By the power of Jesus, the Christ, and the velocity of the seven eyes of the Lamb, who are the seven fiery Spirits of Elshaddai, I impeach and condemn by the blood of the Lamb the mystic kingdoms of darkness that are perpetrating evil devices against my family members, and I now deliver my household from combined and perplexing troubles projected from the occult altars of the trenches of the oceans, the plains of the deserts, the burrows of the forest, and the axis of the air.

You said in Psalms 50:15, **"And call upon Me in the day of trouble; and I will deliver you, and you shall honor Me."** Now O Lord Jesus, hide my household within cylinders of fire, for it is written in Psalms 27:5, **"For in the time of trouble he shall hide me in his pavilion: in the secret of his tabernacle shall he hide me; he shall set me up upon a rock".**

I rain snare of fire upon every satanic and diabolic power working with occult techniques and formulas to destroy my household through consecutive troubles, so that it will no longer resemble the role model of a good family; I dispel this curse and demonic manipulation, and I banish this spirit who is earnestly seeking to decharacterized my household.

I renounce and rebuke every atmospheric disturbance that is in the atmosphere of my household, and astral poisons that are charged with the mandate to induce and forge consecutive household problems.

Destroy their plots and evil plans Lord Jesus, and scatter and destroy them by swords of fire, for it is written in 2 Kings 19:35, **"And it came to pass that night, that the angel of the LORD went out, and smote in the camp of the Assyrians a hundred fourscore and five thousand: and when they arose early in the morning, behold, they *were* all dead corpses."**

I pray today, by the righteousness and judgement that surround the sapphire throne of God, let mass destruction fall upon any witch, warlock, Satanist, ritualist, grand master, ascending master, shaman, witch doctor, native doctor, wise man, avatar, ascended master, mermaid, siren, voodoo priests who are maneuvering combined elemental witchcraft and are programmed to strike my household with chronic severe problems of various sorts.
It is written in Psalms 138:7, **"Though I walk in the midst of trouble, thou wilt revive me: thou shalt stretch forth thine hand against the wrath of mine enemies, and thy right hand shall save me."**

Let these evil occult agents and beings be confronted, apprehended, and neutralized by the unquenchable fire of disastrous proportions, now in Jesus' name.
Psalms 143:11 says, **"Quicken me, O LORD, for thy name's sake: for thy righteousness' sake bring my soul out of trouble."**

O Lord, deliver my household from the elemental demons of selfishness, quick to argue, slow to listen, but quick to wrath. Let all spiritual structures constructed to manipulate the behaviors of my household, in order to cause additional household problems, be dismantled by lightning mixed with fire by Your eternal power.

Your word says in Psalms 34:7, **"The angel of the LORD encamps around those who fear Him and delivers them."**
As well as in Psalms 91:11, it says, **"For he shall give his angels charge over thee, to keep thee in all thy ways."**

Father, lift any financial burdens that weigh heavily on our minds and hearts. We know that money problems can create stress, division, and anxiety, but we rebuke these tactics of the kingdom of darkness. I ask for your provision and wisdom in managing the resources You have entrusted to us. We pray that you would open doors of opportunity for us to thrive financially, while teaching us to be good stewards of what we have. Help us to trust in Your ability to provide for all our needs, and to remain patient and faithful as we wait for Your answers.

I pray against false opportunities that are sent to entrap my household, and every power of darkness that came to steal, kill, and destroy; let the Lord God rebuke the hand of the five continental dragons, the dragons of space, and the dragons of the waters for the sake of my household.

I come up against the demons of grudges, resentment, bitterness, indifference, dissatisfaction, and discord so that peace can reign in my household.

I ask You to heal the hearts, relationships, and destiny of the members of my household by your light and fire and restore to my immediate family circle the spirit of unity and harmony by the blood of the altar of the mercy seat.
Give my household the capacity to embrace love, patience, and kindness in order to ward off the influences and temptations of psychological and emotional problems.
Replace the sadness and regret with Your joy, and may Your love overflow in our hearts so that we can forgive each other as You have forgiven us.

Lord, we ask for Your intervention in any strained relationships within my household and let the God of reconciliation bring the glory of peace and restoration, unconditional love, and understanding in order to build each other up. Where there is division, bring unity.

Where there is hurt, bring healing. Where there is confusion, bring clarity. Where there is darkness, bring light, and where there is sadness, bring joy. Where there is lack, bring bounty. Where there is weeping and sorrow, bring laughter and feasting. Where there has been strife, may peace abound. Where there has been confusion, may clarity reign. Where there has been anger, may love and understanding prevail.

Lord Jesus, I call for angelic assistance to invade my atmosphere with the virtues of your Holy Spirit. Destroy all channels by which the demons of household troubles are prone to come in because of the gate of past hurts, misunderstandings, unmet needs, brokenness in our hearts, tensions between siblings, misunderstandings between spouses, or challenges with extended family members.

Therefore, I speak by fire into the astral layers and planes, and I say, all household problems designed to cloud our judgment and actions, and reconfigure the attitude of my household negatively, be neutralized and banished now, in Jesus' name.

I take authority by fire in the name of Jesus, and I bring into subjection the powers of the twelve gates of hell targeting our hearts, our minds, and our relationships with division, trouble, and strife.
I say all things that serve as doorways to invite the spirit of household problems into my family, be trucked by the arrows of the presence of God's judgement.

Lord, we ask for Your wisdom and discernment as we navigate the challenges of family life. Help us to communicate with each other in love and understanding, to be patient when things are difficult, and to listen more than we speak. When conflicts arise, give us the humility to seek reconciliation and the courage to apologize when necessary. May we always seek peace and work toward solutions that honour You and one another.

O Lord, heal by the stripes of Christ the emotional wounds that have been inflicted upon members of my household, to keep us safe from harm, from negative influences, and from anything that could disrupt the peace of my household.

Build a fortress and fortitude around my household, and may my home be a place of refuge, where Your presence is felt and Your peace reigns. May my household reflect Your goodness and grace, and may it be a place where all who enter feel Your love, peace, and presence.

Lord, we ask for Your supernatural peace to settle over our household. We know that You are the Prince of Peace, and we invite You into every corner of our home. Let Your peace guard our hearts and minds in Christ Jesus, and may it overflow into every area of our lives.

We also pray for patience, Lord, in the midst of daily struggles. We know that the pressures of work, school, finances, and life can easily cause us to become frustrated, irritable, or overwhelmed. Help us to slow down, to take a breath, and to trust in Your timing. Remind us that You are in control, and that Your plans for us are always good.

May we find comfort and strength in knowing that You are with us through every challenge we face.

In all these things, we place our trust in You, knowing that You are faithful and just. We pray that You would heal, restore, and strengthen our household so that we may glorify You in all that we do.

May Your will be done in our lives, and may we walk in Your peace and joy every day; in Jesus' name, we pray, Amen and Amen.

16. BRING THE CASES OF YOUR HOUSEHOLD'S TO THE COURTS OF HEAVEN

Your royal Highness, Heavenly Father I enter your courts with thanksgiving and into your gates with praise. I come boldly before the throne of grace to obtain mercy and find grace to help in my time of need(scripture).

I bless you and I worship you. You alone are my God, and I choose to serve you forever. Let everything that has breadth praise the Lord. I praise you Almighty God, I praise you Lord Jesus, and I praise the Holy Spirit.

Heavenly Father, you are the Judge of Heaven and Earth. I enter into your courtroom in humility and reverence of your Holy name. I stand before you because you instructed me to come boldly before you whenever I need help and also for me to receive mercy. I stand before you Judge of Heaven and Earth cloth in the garment of the righteousness given to me in Christ Jesus through His blood that was shed for me and the covenant of His promises for those who believe in Him.
I welcome my King the Lord Jesus Christ, the Holy Spirit, and the Cloud of witnesses chosen by the Judge of Heaven and Earth for this court case. I also call in the accuser who has accusations against me and my bloodlines.

Presentation of the case & Repentance

I am here to present my case concerning the day of my birth (mention the date here) _________ and I also ask for a divorce and severance between me and the evil and wickedness in my bloodline on both sides of my parents that was passed down from generations to generations. You said if we ask for the forgiveness of our sins, you are faithful to forgive us and cleanse us from all unrighteousness (scripture here). You also said you are the God the I AM that I Am. You forgive iniquity, you forgive sin, and you forgive transgressions (Exo 33).

I want to confess all the acts of evil and wickedness in my bloodline on both sides of my parents down to the time and generations of Adam and Eve. I ask King Yeshua to open my books and the books of my ancestors concerning this case.

I make it right with my accuser quickly in the natural realm, concerning every accusation written down before this court according to your word that says to agree with the adversary quickly while on the way to court (Matt 5:25).

I confess that I and my parents and ancestors have committed these sins and the acts of evil and wickedness against you, God of Heaven and Earth and against other humans and your creations. I ask for your mercy and grace to cover me, and I repent of these sins, iniquities, and transgressions in the name of Jesus.

I call on the blood of Jesus to wash and cleanse me and my bloodlines of the sins in Jesus' name. I also call on the blood of Jesus to break the consequences and ramifications that came into my life/our lives because of our sins.

I ask Father, that the consequences of the sin will no longer be used by the enemy against me (household etc) in any area of my life in Jesus' name. I would also like to request that all the accusations be erased and wiped off by the blood of Jesus Christ from the books in Heaven and those written down by the enemy in the courtroom of hell and the kingdom of darkness or anywhere else.

I make this request in humility based on the law of your Kingdom that if the Son of God shall set you free, you shall be free indeed (scriptures). You also stated in the law of your Kingdom that Yeshua was wounded for our transgressions, He was bruised for our iniquities, the punishment that brought us peace was upon Him and by His stripes we were healed and made whole (Isaiah 53). I ask for your peace, healing, and wholeness to come upon me as stated in your word and statutes in Jesus' name.

I thank you for forgiving me of my sins, and iniquities and cleansing me of my unrighteousness.

[Present the day of your conception and birth before the court]
Heavenly Father, I would like to call the day of my conception and birth to come into the courtroom. I would also like to call the Angel that you appointed for me to come into the Courtroom of Heaven and to stand before you (Scriptures: Job 1, Job10:10, Matt.18:10, Psalm 103:20, Psalm 34:7).

Heavenly Father, I would like to request that the day of my conception be aligned with your will and purpose for my life. I call on the blood of Jesus to stand as a wall of protection between my conception and all evil and wickedness coming through my bloodline on both sides of my parents.
I ask Lord Jesus for your holiness and righteousness and your blood to be poured over the date of my conception and the day of my birth in that timeline.

I renounce and reject all iniquities in the bloodline. I renounce the sin and curses passed down through the bloodline from generations past. I reject them from getting transferred to me. Lord Jesus, you were there when I was conceived because you are omnipresent, and nothing is hidden in your sight. I ask that you wrap me in your light and keep my conception and birth under the shadow of your wings.

I ask for my Angel/s that you have assigned to help me in my journey on earth to be clothed with the nourishments they need and given all the equipment and weapons they need for the work that you have appointed them to do in my life. If my Angel/s are bound by the enemy in the regions of captivity, I humbly ask for your mighty warring Angels to be assigned for them to rescue them from the net of the enemy (Dan.10:13-14) and the evil regions where they have been captured. I ask that you align my Angels back into your assignment that you have appointed them to accomplish in my life (household etc).

Judgment against the enemy, strongman, cohorts, familiar spirits, and familial spirits
Heavenly Father, I would like to request your judgment against the ungodly spirit of evil and wickedness in my bloodline on both sides of my parents. According to the law of your Kingdom that the evil of the wicked must come to an end, but you will establish the righteous (Psalm 7:9).

I also stand on your word in Psalm 149:6-9(read the scriptures in the courtroom) for your judgment against this ungodly spirit, the strongman, cohorts, familiar and familial spirits in Jesus' name. I also ask that the seal be broken from the sealing demon and the strongman, and all their groups and gangs be bound with chains and fetters of iron and judged according to Psalm 149:6-9.

Annulment of evil covenants, cancelations of all evil promises, oaths, and vows. Separation from the evil/agents of the kingdom of darkness in the bloodline. Build a new altar to God and anoint it in the name of the Father, Son, and Holy Spirit.
Heavenly Father, I would also like to request for an annulment of all evil covenants made on my behalf before I was conceived or made by me consciously or subconsciously to be annulled according to your word in Isaiah 28:13-18.

Just as you commanded Gideon in Judges 6 to destroy the altar of Baal and cut down the Asherah pole beside it. I stand on that word and ask for your Angelic assistance for the destruction of the evil altar of wickedness in my bloodline on both sides of my parents. I also by faith smash the evil altar and cut down the Asherah pole beside it. I renounce the evil altars in my life and the demon/strongman attached to them. Heavenly Father, I now build a new altar to your name just as you commanded Gideon to build a new altar to you to replace the evil altar.

By faith, I build this altar to you and call the altar Jehovah T'sidkenu, the God My Righteousness. I anoint this new altar in the name of the Father, the Son, and the Holy Spirit.
I also ask Heavenly Father for divorce and separation between me and (you can mention their names here if you know them) in my bloodline on both sides of my parents who continue to open doors for the enemy through the practice of divination, sorcery, occult, witchcraft, worship of the dead, and so on.

I ask the court to separate me/my children/my descendants/lineage from any spiritual connection between us. I also ask for a separation and divorce between me and any evil flowing from my bloodline on both sides of my parents. I claim all the blessings that you have poured into my bloodline, and I reject the evil planted there by the enemy.

Light and darkness do not mix. I am a child of the Kingdom of Light and I will no longer allow the evil from the enemy to come into my life through the activities of those still practicing the acts of the kingdom of darkness. I give back everything in my life that belongs to the kingdom of darkness either transferred to me through the bloodline or that was placed in my life consciously or unconsciously in Jesus' name. I renounce every authority that ___________(name the people/family/tribe etc.) has over me.

Heavenly Father, I also ask for Angelic assistance to take back all the blessings that were taken from me and my bloodline by the enemy in Jesus' name. I cut all ungodly soul ties with him/her/them. I declare that he/she/they will no longer represent me or stand for me at any point in time in the spirit realm or do evil trading on my behalf with the enemy. I forbid this in Jesus' name. I also confess and repent for the times when I was also ignorant and participated in such ungodly acts of ________ (say what it is/was). I ask for your forgiveness in Jesus' name.

I cleanse the timelines and the land/s when the sin was committed with the blood of Jesus. I also break all ungodly soul ties with the land where the sin was committed. I now make a new covenant with Jesus Christ today; I declare before this court my allegiance to Jesus Christ the Son of God. Who is the King of Kings and Lord of Lords. I will only worship Him, and I will only serve Him, I will have no other god besides Him. I make this blood covenant upon His death, resurrection, and His blood that was shed for me on the cross.

Break all curses and declare blessings over your conception and day of birth
By the authority I have in Jesus Christ, I cancel all curses and negative words spoken over me by ________ (name the person/people/tribe). I reverse these curses and negative words in Jesus' name. (Note: Declare the blessings of God to replace the curse and negative words).

I now invoke a Divine Judicial Order from the Courts of the Almighty God who is the Grand Judge of the Heavens and the Earth, and I command by this Divine Judicial Order that there be rest and peace in my family household, with an immediate release of joy unspeakable and full of glory,